Thinking Critically: Stem Cell Research

William Dudley

ReferencePoint Press®

San Diego, CA

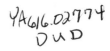

About the Author

William Dudley is the author of several books for ReferencePoint Press, including *Human Rights* and *Unicorns*. A graduate of Beloit College in Wisconsin, he lives in San Diego, California, with his wife and three children.

© 2014 ReferencePoint Press, Inc.
Printed in the United States

For more information, contact:
ReferencePoint Press, Inc.
PO Box 27779
San Diego, CA 92198
www. ReferencePointPress.com

Picture Credits:
Cover credit: Thinkstock Images
Rick Wood/Rapport Press/Newscom: 9
A. Guillotte: 15, 21, 28, 35, 43, 47, 56, 62

LIBRARY OF CONGRESS CATALOGING-IN-PUBLICATION DATA

Dudley, William, 1964-
  Thinking critically. Stem cell research / by William Dudley.
    pages cm. -- (Thinking critically)
  Audience: Grade 9 to 12.
  Includes bibliographical references and index.
  ISBN-13: 978-1-60152-586-4 (hardback)
  ISBN-12: 1-60152-586-9 (hardback)
  1. Stem cells--Research--Government policy--United States--Juvenile literature. 2. Stem cells--Research--Moral and ethical aspects--United States--Juvenile literature. 3. Human embryo--Research--Moral and ethical aspects--United States--Juvenile literature. I. Title. II. Title: Stem cell research.
  QH588.S83D83 2014
  616.02'774072--dc23
                                                                    2013019398

Contents

Foreword   4
Overview: Stem Cell Research   6

Chapter One: Is Embryonic Stem Cell Research Ethical?
The Debate at a Glance   12
Human Embryonic Stem Cell Research Is Not Ethical   13
Human Embryonic Stem Cell Research Is Ethical   19

**Chapter Two: Is Embryonic Stem Cell Research
Still Necessary?**
The Debate at a Glance   25
Research Breakthroughs Have Rendered Embryonic Stem Cell
    Research Unnecessary   26
Embryonic Stem Cell Research Remains Necessary   32

**Chapter Three: Should the Federal Government
Fund Embryonic Stem Cell Research?**
The Debate at a Glance   38
The Federal Government Should Fund Embryonic Stem
    Cell Research   39
The Federal Government Should Not Fund Embryonic Stem
    Cell Research   45

**Chapter Four: Are More Government Regulations
Needed for Stem Cell Research?**
The Debate at a Glance   51
Onerous Government Regulations Are Hampering Progress in
    Stem Cell Research   52
The Government Should Carefully Regulate Stem Cell Research
    and Treatments   58

Source Notes   64
Stem Cell Research Facts   69
Related Organizations and Websites   72
For Further Research   75
Index   77

Foreword

"Literacy is the most basic currency of the knowledge economy we're living in today." Barack Obama (at the time a senator from Illinois) spoke these words during a 2005 speech before the American Library Association. One question raised by this statement is: What does it mean to be a literate person in the twenty-first century?

E.D. Hirsch Jr., author of *Cultural Literacy: What Every American Needs to Know*, answers the question this way: "To be culturally literate is to possess the basic information needed to thrive in the modern world. The breadth of the information is great, extending over the major domains of human activity from sports to science."

But literacy in the twenty-first century goes beyond the accumulation of knowledge gained through study and experience and expanded over time. Now more than ever literacy requires the ability to sift through and evaluate vast amounts of information and, as the authors of the Common Core State Standards state, to "demonstrate the cogent reasoning and use of evidence that is essential to both private deliberation and responsible citizenship in a democratic republic."

The Thinking Critically series challenges students to become discerning readers, to think independently, and to engage and develop their skills as critical thinkers. Through a narrative-driven, pro/con format, the series introduces students to the complex issues that dominate public discourse—topics such as gun control and violence, social networking, and medical marijuana. All chapters revolve around a single, pointed question such as Can Stronger Gun Control Measures Prevent Mass Shootings?, or Does Social Networking Benefit Society?, or Should Medical Marijuana Be Legalized? This inquiry-based approach introduces student researchers to core issues and concerns on a given topic. Each chapter includes one part that argues the affirmative and one part that argues the negative—all written by a single author. With the single-author format the predominant arguments for and against an issue can be synthesized into clear, accessible discussions supported by details and evidence including relevant facts, direct quotes, current examples, and statistical illustrations. All volumes include focus questions to guide students as they read each pro/con discussion, a list of key facts, and an annotated list of related organizations and websites for conducting further research.

The authors of the Common Core State Standards have set out the particular qualities that a literate person in the twenty-first century must have. These include the ability to think independently, establish a base of knowledge across a wide range of subjects, engage in open-minded but discerning reading and listening, know how to use and evaluate evidence, and appreciate and understand diverse perspectives. The new Thinking Critically series supports these goals by providing a solid introduction to the study of pro/con issues.

Stem Cell Research

Japanese scientist Shinya Yamanaka received the Nobel Prize in Medicine in 2012 for his discovery of a way to reprogram ordinary cells to behave like embryonic stem cells. In 2006 he injected special proteins into an adult mouse cell and was able to revert it to its embryonic stem cell (ESCs) form. He repeated the experiment with human cells in 2007.

Yamanaka's research was hailed by the Nobel Prize Committee for revolutionizing the science of cellular biology and laying the groundwork for medical breakthroughs. His work was also widely heralded around the world for its ethical implications. "Yamanaka has taken people's ethical concerns seriously about embryo research and modified the trajectory of research into a path that is acceptable for all," argued scientist and ethicist Julian Savulescu about Yamanaka's breakthrough. "He deserves not only a Nobel Prize for Medicine, but a Nobel Prize for ethics."[1]

Human stem cells have been known as a promising avenue for research and medicine since the late 1990s, but stem cell research has been engulfed in controversy. To understand why, and the implications of Yamanaka's work, requires an understanding of what stem cells are, what they can do, and how scientists obtain them for research.

What Are Stem Cells?

Cells are the microscopic building blocks from which all living organisms are made. The human body is composed of trillions of cells. Most of these cells are differentiated, meaning they have developed specialized characteristics that make them skin cells, blood cells, or some other of the more than two hundred cell types biologists have identified within the human body. Differentiated cells have limited powers to replicate themselves; some types do not replicate at all, while others can replicate the same specialized type.

Stem cells differ from these specialized cells in two fundamental ways. First, they have an almost unlimited capacity for self-replication. A line of stem cells isolated in the laboratory can keep regenerating itself to produce millions of identical copies. Second, stem cells are unspecialized, or undifferentiated, and thus have the capability to produce multiple types of specialized, tissue-specific cells. This characteristic is known as plasticity.

> "[Shinya] Yamanaka has taken people's ethical concerns seriously about embryo research and modified the trajectory of research into a path that is acceptable for all."[1]
>
> —Scientist and ethicist Julian Savulescu.

According to the National Institutes of Health (NIH), "When a stem cell divides, each new cell has the potential either to remain a stem cell or become another type of cell with a more specialized function, such as a muscle cell, a red blood cell, or a brain cell."[2]

These two characteristics of stem cells—self-replication and plasticity—have made them attractive for several different types of scientific research. Scientists hope to be able to cultivate and train stem cells to become specialized cells to regenerate or repair diseased or injured tissues in people. Scientists also see much potential in using stem cells to research how diseases and genetic conditions occur at a cellular level.

Types of Stem Cells

The two major kinds of stem cells found in nature are embryonic stem cells (ESCs) and adult stem cells. These types of stem cells differ in their abilities and limitations.

Embryonic stem cells come from human embryos that are four or five days old. At that point the original fertilized egg has divided into a pinhead-sized ball called a blastocyst. It has between 150 and 200 cells, divided into an inner and outer layer. If attached to a woman's uterus, the outer layer of the blastocyst becomes the placenta and amniotic fluid, and the inner layer of cells provides all the cells that eventually make up an embryo (and a baby, if the pregnancy is carried to term).

Since 1998, scientists have been able to extract the inner cells of blastocysts and cultivate them in artificial environments. In such cases, the cells do not divide and differentiate into specialized cells and turn into an embryo; instead, they divide and multiply as identical stem cells. These stem cell lines can be frozen for storage or shared with other scientists. However, the fact that the blastocyst is destroyed when used to create ESCs has made this research ethically problematic for many.

Adult stem cells are undifferentiated cells that are found in small numbers in human tissues and organs. They can also be harvested from umbilical cord blood when a baby is born. Adult stem cells are believed to reside in specific areas of the body and remain quiescent, or nondividing, until they are activated by illness or injury. At that point they can create different cells of the tissue type in which they reside. Stem cells in bone marrow, for example, can create different kinds of blood cells but not nerve or skin cells. They are also more difficult to cultivate in the lab. However, the fact that no human eggs or embryos are harmed or tampered with has led many opponents of embryonic stem cell research to tout adult stem cells as an ethically superior alternative.

Presidential Decisions on Stem Cell Research

Since 1998, when human embryonic stem cells were first isolated in the laboratory, stem cell research has been a flashpoint for political controversy. Some have opposed ESC research—or at least government funding of such research—on the grounds that human embryos are destroyed in the process. They contend that ESC research is illegal under a 1995 federal law known as the Dickey-Wicker Amendment. This law specifically forbids federal funding of research that harms or destroys embryos. Others have argued that the destruction of potential human embryos should be weighed against the potential for new cures and treatments, and that the Dickey-Wicker Amendment does not apply to research on human stem cells. The controversy has led the two most recent US presidents to issue special executive orders concerning stem cell research.

In August 2001 President George W. Bush approved federal funding for ESC research but with restrictions. The primary restriction authorized federal funding only for research using stem cell lines created prior to Bush's executive order. No federal funds could be used to create new human stem cell lines, and stem cell lines created after 2001 (even with

Japanese scientist Shinya Yamanaka researches human stem cells in his lab. Yamanaka received the Nobel Prize in Medicine in 2012 for his discovery of a way to reprogram ordinary cells to behave like embryonic stem cells.

private funds) would be ineligible for use in federally funded research projects. The rationale was to prevent the federal government from creating any incentive for new acts of what many viewed as destruction of human life.

Critics of Bush's policy argued that it severely stinted US progress in stem cell research. When Bush issued his order, sixty stem cell lines existed but only twenty-one proved usable for research. Bush vetoed several attempts by Congress to permit more federal funding of ESC research. Several states during this time attempted to fill the gap in federal funding with their own programs. The largest such effort was in California, where voters passed a 2004 initiative borrowing $3 billion for stem cell research and creating the California Institute for Regenerative Medicine.

Bush was succeeded as president by Barack Obama in 2009. During his campaign Obama had promised to overturn Bush's policy on stem cell research, which he did by issuing his own executive order in March 2009. Obama's order lifted the limit Bush had placed on federal funding of stem cell research. He also ordered the NIH to devise and implement new guidelines on stem cell lines derived from leftover embryos in fertility clinics. The creation of ESC lines would still be off-limits for federal funding, but post-2001 stem cell lines could be used for federal research projects. By 2012 the NIH had approved and made available 182 ESC lines for research.

> "When a stem cell divides, each new cell has the potential either to remain a stem cell or become another type of cell with a more specialized function, such as a muscle cell, a red blood cell, or a brain cell."[2]
>
> —National Institutes of Health, US government agency charged with medical research.

Yamanaka and a New Source of Stem Cells

Prior to Obama's reversal, the stem cell research field had already been rocked by Yamanaka's discovery. Working first with mouse cells, then human cells, Yamanaka was able to transform an ordinary (nonstem) differentiated cell into one with most of the characteristics of ESCs. His discovery became known as induced pluripotent stem (iPS) cells, which have become popular for research on human development and disease. Like ESCs, iPS cells are pluripotent, meaning they can potentially develop into any sort of cell. But unlike ESCs, they can be created without harming or destroying blastocysts or embryos.

But whether iPS cells have fully resolved all the ethical controversies over stem cell research remains unclear. Whereas some scientists and policy makers argue that advances in iPS cells mean that ESC research is no longer necessary and should be halted, others argue that all types of stem cell research should be supported (and funded). Disagreements exist on how strictly stem cell research—and stem cell medical therapies—should be regulated by the government. Stem cell research remains a fount of both great potential and great controversy.

Chapter One

Is Embryonic Stem Cell Research Ethical?

Human Embryonic Stem Cell Research Is Not Ethical

- The process of creating ESCs destroys human embryos.
- Human embryos are human lives.
- Potential benefits to patients do not justify the means of destroying human lives.
- Stem cell research raises troubling questions about human cloning.

The Debate at a Glance

Human Embryonic Stem Cell Research Is Ethical

- The cell clusters used in research are not equivalent to a human life.
- Human embryonic stem cell research has the potential to greatly help many people.
- Embryonic stem cells can be obtained from unused in vitro fertilization (IVF)–clinic embryos, which would otherwise be destroyed.
- Embryonic stem cell research operates under ethical overview and guidelines.

Human Embryonic Stem Cell Research Is Not Ethical

"Many people have legitimate concerns with the destruction of human life for human embryonic stem cell treatments. Medical science must be about protecting human life, not ending it."

—Right to Life of Michigan, an antiabortion organization.

Right to Life of Michigan, "iPSCs—Advances in Ethical Stem Cell Research," 2012. http://media.rtl.org.

Consider these questions as you read:

1. What fundamental ethical principles are being cited to question the ethics of human embryonic stem cell research? Do you believe these principles are applicable to this issue? Why or why not?
2. What reasoning did President George W. Bush use to justify his restrictions on ESC research? Do you agree or disagree with his rationale? Explain.
3. How central is the belief that human life begins at conception to the ethical critique of stem cell research? Explain your answer.

Editor's note: The discussion that follows presents common arguments made in support of this perspective, reinforced by facts, quotes, and examples taken from various sources.

Just because something *can* be done does not mean it *should* be done. A worthy end is not justified by immoral means. These fundamental principles apply to scientific endeavors as much as to any part of human life. The tools that biologists have developed for isolating and creating ESC lines raise serious ethical concerns. While proponents tout such research as a potential gold mine of new medical cures and knowledge, these alluring goals do not in the end justify the moral costs of embryonic stem cell research.

The central ethical problem with ESC research is that it involves the destruction of innocent human lives. Embryonic stem cells are the cells created in the early stages of human development after fertilization. The ESC lines used by scientists all come from embryos that were killed in the process of harvesting their cells. "In the minds of many," writes author and biologist Joseph Panno, "a stem cell therapy that requires the destruction of human embryos hark[s] back to the cruel experiments that prisoners were forced to endure at the hands of the Nazis during World War II."[3]

> "In the minds of many, a stem cell therapy that requires the destruction of human embryos hark[s] back to the cruel experiments that prisoners were forced to endure at the hands of the Nazis during World War II."[3]
>
> —Joseph Panno, the author of *Stem Cell Research: Medical Applications and Ethical Controversy.*

Panno was referring to notorious experiments in German concentration camps in which prisoners, for example, were deliberately infected with diseases to test cures or subjected to freezing temperatures to test the body's response to cold. "The association is not as far-fetched as it may first appear," Panno notes, arguing that "problems associated with stem cell research are closely related to the ethical problems affecting biomedical research in general."[4]

Biomedical Ethics and the Belmont Report

The United States has had its own history of medical research atrocities, including the infamous Tuskegee scandal in which hundreds of African American men with syphilis were studied but never informed of their condition or treated. These experiments took place over a period of forty years, from 1932 to 1972. In response to questions raised by the Nazi and Tuskegee scandals, the US Department of Health, Education, and Welfare commissioned a study in 1973 to identify and codify medical ethics. The resulting *Belmont Report*, published in 1976, identified several fundamental principles to govern scientific research on human subjects. One was the principle of beneficence—the idea that research

Why Some People Believe Embryonic Stem Cell Research Is Wrong

A poll by Charlton Research Company asked people who condemned embryonic stem cell research—even for the purpose of curing diseases—the reasons for their disapproval. It found that a majority of opponents cited religion as the basis for their opposition.

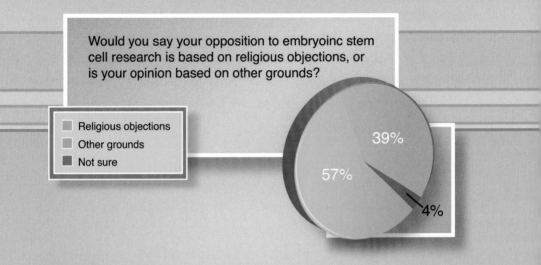

Would you say your opposition to embryoinc stem cell research is based on religious objections, or is your opinion based on other grounds?

- Religious objections
- Other grounds
- Not sure

39%

57%

4%

Source: Charlton Research Company, "Stem Cell Research Public Opinion Statistics," June 20, 2012. www.statisticsbrain.com.

subjects not be deliberately injured or harmed. Another was the notion that participants in human research should, as a matter of justice, be able to reap the benefits of such research. A third was the principle of informed consent—the idea that research subjects must first provide written consent after being informed of details of the experiment in question.

Clearly, ESC research violates all three of these principles in regards to the embryo. An embryo that is destroyed in the process of research is indisputably harmed, does not reap any benefits from the research, and is incapable of giving informed consent.

The *Belmont Report* does not directly address human embryonic stem cell research, which did not exist when the document was written. Nor do its guidelines explicitly ban embryo research since embryos are also not persons in the legal sense. However, that does not mean that the ethical principles outlined in the *Belmont Report* are irrelevant. Whether an embryo becomes a human with full human rights is a long-standing philosophical question. But, as John Yockey, a Roman Catholic friar, reminds us, every human begins as an embryo. "Every human embryo is a genuine good as such, deserving of respect, never a pawn on somebody else's chessboard, never to be used by another as material for human engineering."[5] In other words, human embryos should not be treated as a means to another person's ends—even if those ends are admirable.

"No Such Thing as a Spare Embryo"

This fundamental respect for human life should apply even when dealing with so-called "spare" embryos. Some defenders of ESC research argue that the embryos killed are leftovers from IVF treatments that would never have become babies in any case. However, that is not necessarily true. Couples who go through fertility treatments that result in excess frozen embryos have the option of donating them for adoption. The embryos can be implanted in another woman's womb and grow into children. Between 2004 and 2009 about nineteen hundred infants, called *snowflakes* because they were frozen at one point, were born through this procedure, according to Reginald Finger, the director of an organization that advises families and professionals on embryo donation and adoption. Former president George W. Bush hosted a 2005 White House event with several families with snowflake children. During this event he stated that they "remind us that there is no such thing as a spare embryo" and that "these lives are not raw material to be exploited, but gifts."[6] Donating one's embryos for adoption is an ethically superior choice to donating the embryos to be destroyed in stem cell research.

But if embryo adoption is not possible, is destroying the embryos for research better than simply discarding them? Again former president Bush, recounting his wrestling with stem cell research during his presidency in his memoir *Decision Points*, decided no. "Some argue that these embryos would never become children, and that it is better to use them for research. Yet there is, or ought to be, an ethical boundary between letting embryos die naturally and proactively ending their lives. One should not sanction the destruction of life to save life."[7]

> **"There is no such thing as a spare embryo."[6]**
>
> —George W. Bush, president of the United States from 2001 to 2009.

Human Cloning Is Not an Ethical Option

Some scientists are pursuing an alternative to using donated IVF embryos. Somatic cell nuclear transfer (SCNT) does not involve a fertilized egg. Rather, the nucleus (which contains most of the genetic material) is removed from an unfertilized egg and replaced with the nucleus of an adult cell, such as a skin or muscle cell. The egg is then cultured in the lab to develop into an early-stage embryo and, thus, a source of ESCs. The process has proved easier for animal cells than human cells; after years of false starts, the first successful attempt to create a human embryo via SCNT was announced in May 2013.

However, SCNT creates its own ethical problems. SCNT has been used to create cloned sheep and other animals, and some observers fear it might be tried for human reproduction as well. Some stem cell research apologists have attempted to make a distinction between *reproductive* cloning (which is widely frowned upon) and *therapeutic* cloning, in which only stem cells, not cloned creatures, are created. But therapeutic cloning then means that a human life or embryo has been specifically created only to be destroyed and utilized for its parts. "A cloned human embryo, no less than a human embryo produced by the union of gametes, is an embryonic human. That is a matter of biological fact,"[8] asserts philosophy professor Justin D. Barnard.

Ethical Forms of Stem Cell Research

The ethical questions raised by ESC research do not apply to other forms of stem cell research. Indeed, the fact that alternatives exist to achieve the same ends strengthens the case against embryonic stem cell research. Adult (or tissue-specific) stem cells are stem cells that are found within the human body. They function as a reserve source of new cells. Although they do not have the ability to turn into any and all types of cells, scientists have found them highly promising for research and medical treatments. Adult stem cells have been used in at least seventy medical treatments. They do not require the killing of embryos; they can be taken from a patient with his or her consent.

Another potential source of useful stem cells is found in the umbilical cord blood of newborn infants; many parents have taken the step to preserve umbilical cord blood for that reason. Finally, in 2007 scientists discovered that by adding certain proteins to ordinary skin or other specialized cells, they could reprogram these cells to their embryonic state. These reprogrammed cells (known as induced pluripotent stem cells) have the same potential and promise of embryonic stem cells, but no embryo is destroyed in their creation. All of these methods of stem cell research deserve more public support and attention because they avoid the ethical problems of ESC research and fully live up to the ethical ideals expressed in the *Belmont Report.*

Human Embryonic Stem Cell Research Is Ethical

"The generation of IVF embryos for reproductive purposes necessitates excess embryos that will be stored indefinitely or destroyed. The creation for ethically responsible research of stem cell lines from these . . . embryos that will never be implanted in a womb is a subsequent, determining act that chooses *humanitarian benefit over biomedical waste.*"

—Stem Cell Action Coalition, an organization that supports government funding of human embryonic stem cell research.

Stem Cell Action Coalition, "Talking Points for Stem Cell Research," 2010. http://stemcellaction.org.

Consider these questions as you read:

1. Do you agree or disagree with the view that unused embryos from in vitro fertilization clinics can ethically be used for research? Why or why not?

2. What actions and safeguards have scientists taken to ensure their stem cell research is ethical? Do you believe they are sufficient? Why or why not?

3. How do Andres and Paulina Trevino justify their decision to donate embryos for stem cell research? Would you make a similar decision if you were in this position? Why or why not?

Editor's note: The discussion that follows presents common arguments made in support of this perspective, reinforced by facts, quotes, and examples taken from various sources.

Human embryonic stem cells are found in embryos that are four to five days old and have about 150 cells. At this early stage of development, the embryo is in the shape of a ball called a blastocyst. The outer cells of the ball (the trophoblast) are forerunners of the placenta and other tissues that help with gestation in the uterus. The interior cells (the inner cell mass) contain the embryonic stem cells that, if allowed to develop fully, become a human individual. Or, if they are separated from the trophoblast at this early point, they become a line of human embryonic stem cells. These special cells are pluripotent, meaning they possess the ability to divide into more cells or to develop into any one of the specialized skin, muscle, brain, or other cells that compose the human body. This ability gives these cells enormous potential for use in scientific research and for generating healthy cells to replace diseased cells.

Despite this potential, stem cell research has been controversial since human embryonic cells were first isolated in the laboratory in 1998. Stem cell scientists have been fully aware of the ethical issues and questions raised by their work on human embryos. James A. Thomson, the University of Wisconsin scientist who first cultivated stem cell lines from human embryos, acknowledges the ethical implications. "If human embryonic stem cell research does not make you at least a little bit uncomfortable, you have not thought about it enough."[9]

Steps Taken to Ensure Ethical Research

The stem cell research community has taken numerous steps to ensure that its work does not violate basic rules and ethical guidelines. Universities, hospitals, and other organizations that house such research have special committees (sometimes called embryonic stem cell research oversight committees) that evaluate every proposed stem cell research project to make sure it falls within ethical rules. These committees include scientists, doctors, ethicists, legal experts, and members of the community. Research funded by the NIH must conform to NIH guidelines that were published in 2000 and revised in 2009. Projects not directly funded by the NIH generally may still fall within certain guidelines. For instance, the National Academy of Sciences developed ethical guidelines in 2005 and has since revised them several times. Likewise, the International Society for Stem Cell Research, a nongovernmental organization, published its guidelines in 2006.

These guidelines were generally developed after much discussion and revision. The NIH, for example, received more than forty-nine thousand comments from scientists, universities, patient advocacy groups,

A Majority of Americans Believe Embryonic Stem Cell Research Is Ethical

The Gallup organization conducts an annual "Values and Beliefs" in which they survey a random sample of more than one thousand American adults for their view on various controversial issues. One question in the annual survey asks participants to comment on the morality of medical research using stem cells obtained from human embryos. The year-by-year results charted in this graph reveal that a strong and consistent majority of Americans believe that human embryonic stem cell research is morally acceptable.

Regardless of whether or not you think embryonic stem cell research should be legal, for each one, please tell me whether you personally believe that in general it is morally acceptable or morally wrong. How about medical research using stem cells obtained from human embryos?

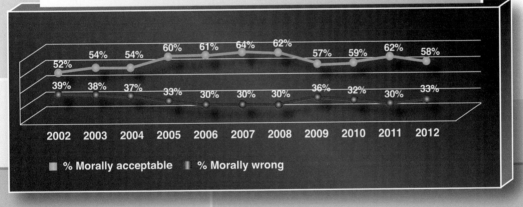

Source: Gallop, "Stem Cell Research," 2012. www.gallop.com.

religious and medical organizations, and private citizens in the course of developing and refining ethical guidelines in 2009. The resulting guidelines limit federally funded research to stem cells derived from embryos "that were created using in vitro fertilization for reproductive purposes and were no longer needed for this purpose."[10] In addition, the donors of the embryos (the people whose sperm and eggs were used to make them) have to give informed and written consent that these embryos can be used for research. The guidelines forbid any cash payments or other coercion for embryo donation. The guidelines also forbid funding of research that creates embryos for the purposes of research through cloning or the mixture of human stem cells with nonhuman cells.

Questions of Moral Standing

However, for some people, these guidelines and institutional safeguards are insufficient. They have an absolutist belief that embryos at all stages of development are human persons and should be accorded the same moral status as infants, children, and adults. Several religious bodies, notably the Catholic Church, hold that each human being is a unique soul from the moment of conception. Thus, because the process of establishing an ESC line terminates the source embryo, they believe that all ESC research is inherently unethical.

However, the idea that embryos have moral standing equal to living persons is not shared by all people—or all religions. "According to Jewish, Islamic, Hindu and Buddhist traditions, as well as many Western Christian views, moral standing arrives much later during the gestation process,"[11] writes bioethics professor Insoo Hyan. The United States is a religiously pluralistic nation, which demands a tolerance for differing religious and personal views on questions such as when embryos develop full moral standing.

It is reasonable to believe that a 150-cell blastocyst does not have the same moral status as a living person. An estimated 75 percent of early embryos conceived in intercourse are naturally lost due to a failure to implant in the womb. Many people believe that embryos that have not implanted and thus not begun the process of cell differentiation should be seen as a collection of human cells but not a human life. This is akin to human cancer cells in a lab, which are human, and are alive, but are not a human life. Others argue that while it may be proper to treat early human embryos with respect, using them for research that advances knowledge and perhaps saves human lives would be a way of showing that respect.

Using Embryos That Would Otherwise Be Discarded

In addition, the ESCs used in research are virtually all derived, as per NIH guidelines, from leftover embryos stored in fertility clinics. Scientist Lawrence S.B. Goldstein and Meg Schneider, of the University of California at San Diego, note that "Fertility clinics have as many as 400,000 blastocysts stored in freezers, many of which will never be used to start a pregnancy and will eventually be destroyed, regardless of whether they are used for research."[12]

In this case, scientists are not creating life to destroy it but are utilizing a resource that would otherwise be lost. Thomson, the Wisconsin researcher whose team first isolated human embryonic stem cells, said in a 2005 interview that "regardless of what you think the moral status of those embryos is, it makes sense to me that it's a better moral decision to use them to help people than to just throw them out."[13]

> "Regardless of what you think the moral status of those embryos is, it makes sense to me that it's a better moral decision to use them to help people than to just throw them out."[13]
>
> —James A. Thomson, the scientist who first isolated human embryonic stem cell lines.

One Family's Story

The choice of donation lies entirely with the couple who created the embryo. Andres and Paulina Trevino are one such couple. The Trevinos have a son, named Andy, who was born with a very rare genetic condition (called NEMO) that caused his immune system to fail. "Andy had infections all over his body with different types of bacteria and viruses," Andres explains. "He had no tools to fight them. He had infection in his central nervous system, stomach, skin, eyes, blood and elsewhere."[14]

The only proposed cure was a bone marrow stem cell transplant. However, success depended on donor compatibility. The Trevinos waited for two and a half years in vain for a match. At some point it was suggested that they could create their own match for Andy by having a second child, whose stem cells would be compatible. "But we ran the risk of having another baby with NEMO," Andres recalled, "and on top of that, only one out of four siblings would be compatible with Andy."[15]

They decided to use in vitro fertilization to produce embryos and preimplantation genetic diagnosis to make sure the new child would be

NEMO-free and be compatible with Andy. After screening thirty-six embryos, they found a suitable one and placed it in Paulina's uterus. Six months after Sofia was born, stem cells were removed from her bone marrow and readied for transplant. "After almost 1,000 days of hospitalization in Mexico City and Boston, a stem cell bone marrow transplant cured Andy,"[16] says Andres.

> "We believe that embryonic stem cell research will revolutionize medicine and provide treatments to many life-threatening diseases."[17]
>
> —Andres Trevino, who, with his wife, donated thirty-five embryos from their fertility treatment program for use in embryonic stem cell research.

But what about the remaining thirty-five embryos? The Trevinos donated them to the Stem Cell Research Program at Children's Hospital Boston, where Andy had been treated. They later learned that at least two stem cell lines were successfully created from their donation. The cells have the potential to help other children with life-threatening diseases who are still waiting for compatible stem cells for transplant. Even if those embryos had been destroyed, the Trevinos believe their decision was something that supported human life. Andres says, "We believe that embryonic stem cell research will revolutionize medicine and provide treatments to many life-threatening diseases . . . just as Sofia's stem cells allowed Andy to fight infections and lead a normal life."[17]

Chapter Two

Is Embryonic Stem Cell Research Still Necessary?

Research Breakthroughs Have Rendered Embryonic Stem Cell Research Unnecessary

- Adult stem cells can be harvested from the body.
- Induced stem cells are created from regular body cells.
- Both adult and induced stem cells avoid the problem of killing human embryos.
- Biomedical researchers and funders are turning away from embryonic stem cells.

The Debate at a Glance

Embryonic Stem Cell Research Remains Necessary

- Embryonic stem cells are needed as benchmarks to study other types of stem cells.
- Those who say ESC research is unneeded have ideological reasons for opposing such research.
- Valuable knowledge would be lost if ESC research were no longer supported.
- All types of stem cell research should be pursued to maximize success.

Research Breakthroughs Have Rendered Embryonic Stem Cell Research Unnecessary

"Scientific breakthroughs have rendered embryonic stem-cell research obsolete, effectively removing any perceived need to destroy human embryos in the name of science."

—Mike Pence, Republican governor of Indiana and former member of Congress.

Mike Pence, "The Empty Promise of Embryonic Stem Cell Research," *Christianity Today*, March 23, 2009. www.christianitytoday.com.

Consider these questions as you read:

1. Why is the idea of induced pluripotent stem cells attractive to some opponents of embryonic stem cell research? Do you agree with this view? Why or why not?
2. At what point should scientists (in any field) consider abandoning one form of research in favor of others? Explain your answer.
3. Ian Wilmut, famous for cloning a sheep, has said that scientists should pursue alternatives to human embryonic stem cell research. Does his renown as a scientist lend particular weight to this view? How much?

Editor's note: The discussion that follows presents common arguments made in support of this perspective, reinforced by facts, quotes, and examples taken from various sources.

Human embryonic stem cell research has been controversial ever since 1998, when the first such cells were successfully cultivated at a University of Wisconsin laboratory under biologist James A. Thomson. Cells harvested from early embryos are valued because of their pluripotency, or the ability to develop into any other kind of specialized human cell. But they are also controversial because many people question the morality of destroying embryos to obtain such cells. The result has been an ongoing controversy on how to balance that concern against the research and medical potential of these cells. But suppose there was a way to get all the benefits of human embryonic stem cell research through a different path—one that did not necessitate embryo destruction. Wouldn't that make ESC research—and its troublesome ethical issues—unnecessary?

New Discovery Eliminates Ethical Cloud

Such a path has been blazed by 2012 Nobel Prize winner Shinya Yamanaka. The Japanese scientist wondered if there was a way to take a skin cell or other regular body cell and somehow treat it so it would revert to an embryonic stage of development. After several years of research he announced in 2006 that he had developed a way to reprogram mouse fibroblasts (cells found in connective tissue) into something very similar to embryonic stem cells. By introducing four specific genes, ordinary cells were changed into pluripotent cells that could develop into all different cell types. Within a year, such induced pluripotent stem (iPS) cells were successfully created with human cells. Biologist Thomson, announcing his own experimental success in creating human iPS cells in 2007, said they met the defining criteria of human embryonic stem cells.

Their discovery was quickly recognized as significant. Human iPS cells, many believe, could be used in the same ways that scientists had envisioned using embryonic cells for research into genetic diseases, drug testing, and regenerative medicine. However, they also had at least three advantages that potentially make the use of ESCs all but obsolete: no ethical controversy, no transplant rejection for patients, and relative ease of manufacture.

Yamanaka and Thomson have found a new way of fashioning pluripotent cells without tampering with or destroying human embryos. By creating the "functional equivalent of stem cells," argues Baptist ethicist Andy Lewis, these researchers have provided "great hope for a scientific solution that provides both protection of innocent life and life-saving medical technologies."[18] Induced pluripotent stem cells do not have the ethical cloud (and political controversy) that rightly surrounds ESC research.

A Good Alternative to Embryonic Stem Cells

Many scientists are excited about the potential of induced pluripotent stem (iPS) cells. Such cells share most of the properties of embryionic stem (ES) cells, including the ability to give rise to all the different types of body cells. Scientists involved in iPS cell research say these cells have advantages over embryonic stem cells.

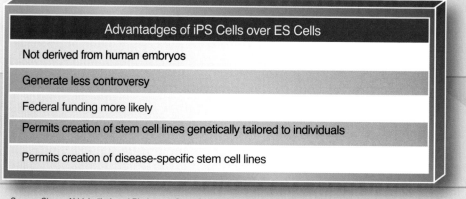

Advantadges of iPS Cells over ES Cells
Not derived from human embryos
Generate less controversy
Federal funding more likely
Permits creation of stem cell lines genetically tailored to individuals
Permits creation of disease-specific stem cell lines

Source: Sigma-Aldrich, "Induced Pluripotent Stem Cell FAQs," 2013. www.sigmaaldrich.com.

Donor Compatibility

In addition to bypassing the controversy surrounding embryos, human iPS cell lines have the advantage of compatibility with the donor of the original skin cell. The potential of using stem cells to create new cells, tissues, or even organs is complicated by the body's rejection of anything foreign. All existing human embryonic stem cell lines are derived from leftover or discarded embryos that would have a different genetic makeup from any non-donor patient. For this reason, the risk of transplant rejection is high.

Human iPS cells can also be more useful than embryonic stem cells for translational research—that is, research that "translates" basic data into information useful for specific uses or treatments. Scientists seeking to learn how the genetic disorder Parkinson's disease changes brain cells, for instance, cannot dissect a patient's brain or even extract affected cells for study. But if they could take a skin cell from a person with Parkinson's and reprogram it into a stem cell line that could then become brain cell tissue, the genetic basis of that disease for that individual could be studied at a cellular level. Similar research using ESCs is hampered by genetic incompatibility and a relative dearth of such cell lines available for study. Induced pluripotent stem cells have supplanted ESCs in this area of research.

A Simpler Alternative

Prior to 2006, the only path to creating ESCs that were genetically compatible with a patient was a process called somatic cell nuclear transfer (SCNT), or cloning. This technique involves taking the nucleus out of an egg cell and replacing it with the nucleus of a regular adult or somatic cell. That cell then becomes the starting point for creating an embryo and harvesting its cells. This technique has been used to clone animal stem cells, but it is expensive and inefficient; it can take hundreds of attempts to produce an ESC line. Scientists toiled for more than a decade to clone human embryos before a team at Oregon Science and Health University announced in 2013 that they had created human ESCs with this technique.

By that time scientists had another source for such cells, making human SCNT unnecessary, argues Australian physician David van Gend. That alternative is iPS cells. "There is no longer any valid reason to attempt cloning to create ES cells because the goal of 'patient-matched pluripotent stem cells,' . . . has been achieved by the iPS cell alternative."[19]

Even without human cloning, iPS cells have proved to be easier to produce then human embryonic stem cells derived from discarded frozen embryos. Embryos need to be legally procured, and extracting their cells is a labor-intensive and expensive process that is not always successful in creating a stem

> "Making human ES cells is a pain."[20]
>
> —James A. Thomson, the stem cell researcher at the University of Wisconsin who first isolated human stem cells in 1998.

cell line. "Making human ES cells is a pain,"[20] noted Thomson, the researcher who first isolated such cells, when interviewed about his own laboratory's transition to focus on human iPS cells instead. By contrast, making iPS cells is simple enough that "a high school lab can do it,"[21] according to stem cell scientist Mehendra Rao.

As a result, stem cell research using iPS cells has exploded. Japan is setting up a special stem cell bank with around seventy-five iPS cell lines for use in possible future therapies. Thomson's own laboratory in Wisconsin has not created a single new human embryonic stem cell line since 2007. "But we've derived dozens if not hundreds of human induced pluripotent stem cells,"[22] he told a reporter in 2013.

Direct Programming

Even as research into iPS cells has accelerated, biomedical scientists have developed other new techniques that eliminate the need for stem cells entirely. In a relatively new method, called direct programming, scientists use techniques somewhat similar to those developed by Yamanaka to reprogram a skin cell directly into a different specialized cell—skipping the stem cell stage altogether. In 2010 scientists were able to take mouse fibroblast cells and reprogram them directly into nerve cells. By 2013 scientists in San Diego had announced that they had successfully turned skin cells into functional neurons (brain cells) by blocking production of a protein. "Direct conversion of skin cells to neurons would take less time than using stem cells as an intermediary, and might be potentially safer,"[23] writes journalist Bradley J. Fikes.

> "Direct conversion of skin cells to neurons would take less time than using stem cells as an intermediary, and might be potentially safer."[23]
>
> —Bradley J. Fikes, a science journalist for the *San Diego Union-Tribune.*

The promise of direct programming has led famed stem cell scientist Ian Wilmut (the man who cloned Dolly the sheep) to tell scientists at a 2011 talk in La Jolla, California, that they should forgo ESC research entirely. He argued that direct programming would provide the same benefits as ESC research (the creation of usable cells) without donor incompatibility risks, and that government funding for embryonic research would likely be limited once safer methods were available. ESC research has effectively been rendered obsolete, according to Wilmut.

The Exception to the Rule

In a way, stem cell research may be the happy exception to the concept that scientific advances create ethical dilemmas. While human embryonic stem cell research has been controversial since its beginnings in 1998, advances in stem cell research may have resolved some of these ethical dilemmas by delivering the benefits of stem cell research without the ethical shadow of destroying human embryos. For both ethical and practical reasons, iPS cells and direct programming of cells promise to make human embryonic stem cell research obsolete.

Embryonic Stem Cell Research Remains Necessary

"Continued research on *all types of stem cells is critical* to developing research strategies that will ultimately provide new therapies."

—International Society for Stem Cell Research, a professional body of stem cell scientists.

International Society for Stem Cell Research, "ISSCR Reaffirms Support for All Forms of Stem Cell Research," press release, October 11, 2012. www.isscr.org.

Consider these questions as you read:

1. Do you believe ideological concerns have affected whether people believe ESC research remains necessary? Why or why not?

2. Do scientists directly involved in stem cell research possess greater credibility or objectivity in their views, in your opinion? Why or why not?

3. Do you believe ESC research can be categorically separated from other types of stem cell research? Why or why not?

Editor's note: The discussion that follows presents common arguments made in support of this perspective, reinforced by facts, quotes, and examples taken from various sources.

Is embryonic stem cell research something whose time has passed? Those who oppose all research involving embryos have been quick to pronounce its imminent demise. Matt Bowman, a lawyer who helped lead a legal challenge to federal funding of ESC research, wrote in 2010 that the technology "dates back to the Stone Age in today's pace of science," and dismissively stated that "embryonic stem cell research should go back to the dinosaur museum where it belongs."[24]

Bowman and others point to iPS cells as an ethically superior alternative that makes ESC research unnecessary. However, this simplistic position betrays misunderstanding both of the potential of ESC research and the process of scientific research itself.

On the Brink of Major Developments

Abandoning ESC research would jeopardize the progress scientists have made in following several tantalizing leads toward treatments and cures. It would be a setback for Marcus Hilton, for example. In January 2012 the thirty-four-year-old British man, who suffers from a degenerative eye disease, had his right eye injected with fifty thousand cells of retinal pigment epithelium that were derived from ESCs. Within a few months he was able to discern improvements in his vision. Robert Lanza, the chief scientific officer of the company holding the clinical trial, said another test patient could "now read her watch"[25]—something she could not do before.

The positive experiences of Hilton may soon be shared by others. Writing in October 2012, Ed Fallone, president of Wisconsin Stem Cell Now, says that "no fewer than fourteen human trials using human embryonic stem cells are expected to seek approval from the Food and Drug Administration (FDA) over the next twenty months."[26] Among the possible beneficiaries are people with macular degeneration, diabetes, and heart disease. It would be a foolhardy gamble at this stage to assume that iPS cells would serve just as well.

Even if it were true that treatments done by ESCs could someday be done with human iPS cells, it would take years before their benefits would reach the clinical trial stage. People such as Marcus Hilton would suffer unnecessary delays in getting medical relief. According to the International Society for Stem Cell Research in an October 2012 statement, "There is considerable value in continuing to develop therapies based on the human ES cell lines that have already been in clinical development for years and have years of analysis and safety information. One cannot replace an existing cell line in research or clinical development without a significant additional investment in time and at considerable additional cost."[27]

Lawrence S.B. Goldstein, the director of the Stem Cell Program at the University of California at San Diego, notes that although human embryonic stem cell research only dates back to 1998, scientists have been working with mouse ESCs for around three decades. Such research "has given them enormously improved understanding of how cells, tissues, organs, and organ systems work in mammals, including humans." The massive body of research has paved the way for similar work involving human embryonic stem cells, he argues. If human embryonic stem cell research "follows the pattern of other science fields with comparable potential, the next 10 to 20 years may well deliver an explosion in discoveries and developments that can reduce human suffering and even save lives."[28]

Potential Problems with iPS Cells

Furthermore, there are serious questions as to whether human iPS cells will ever make it to the human clinical trial stage. Although they are almost identical to human embryonic stem cells, there remain subtle differences between the two types of stem cells—differences that are yet to be fully understood. The original technique of reprogramming cells used viruses to deliver the genes, a procedure that risks the introduction of unwanted and unsafe cell mutations. Several studies have suggested that iPS cells retain a faint imprint of the cell from which they were derived, and they might still trigger unwanted immune system reactions when introduced into test subjects or patients. Lanza, whose company was behind the eye trial using ESCs, has also researched iPS cells. In some experiments, he has found that the iPS cells his team was cultivating aged faster, grew slower, and died at higher rates than cells derived from human embryos. "It would be premature to abandon research using embryonic stem cells until we fully understand what's causing these problems,"[29] he told a journalist.

> "It would be premature to abandon research using embryonic stem cells."[29]
>
> —Robert Lanza, the chief scientific officer of Advanced Cell Technology and a leader in stem cell research.

Michael D. West, the chief executive officer of Biotime, a company involved in stem cell research, offers another justification for contin-

Embryonic Stem Cells Hold Great Promise

Research with embryonic stem (ES) cells offer promising treatments for serious illnesses and the hope of alleviating the suffering of people around the world. While research with other types of stem cells continues, the unique characteristics of human ES cells make them an essential piece of the stem cell research dynamic.

Why Do ES Cells Hold Such Great Promise?
Can develop into any cell type in the body
Can form unlimited quantities of any cell type in the body
Will help us understand inherited diseases by allowing us to study human cells bearing the exact genetic defects that cause disease in patients
Will allow us to discover safer and more effective drugs by making it easier to screen drug candidates

Source: University of Michigan, "Stem Cell Research FAQs: Benefits of Stem Cell Research," 2012. www.stemcellresearch.umich.edu.

ued research and development of ESCs. He argues that human iPS cells might not work for acute disease or injury, such as heart attacks, for the simple reason that it can take weeks to create such cells. "Physicians will not have time to order cells and tissues to be made from the patient's own cells through iPS cell technology." West's company is investing in banks of clinical grade human ES cells for emergency treatment. "The answer that I believe most stem cell researchers would agree upon is that both ES and iPS cells will likely be necessary for a long time."[30]

The Need for Benchmarks

The reprogramming that creates iPS cells is not an exact procedure. For this reason, scientists need benchmarks to determine the success of their efforts to create iPS cells. The benchmark for this work is existing human embryonic stem cells. "Every iPS cell must be thoroughly evaluated before it can be used in any study,"[31] says science writer Monya Baker.

The best way to determine a cell's embryonic stem cell properties is to compare it with an actual embryonic stem cell. "Human ES cells will always be the standard to which other cells will be compared,"[32] says Roger Pederson, a stem cell researcher at Cambridge University in Great Britain.

Francis S. Collins, the head of the NIH, said in congressional testimony that research on iPS cells makes ESC research more, not less, necessary. "Virtually all investigators working in the field agree that additional comparisons between iPS cells and human embryonic stem cells are critically important because human embryonic stem cells remain the gold standard for pluripotency. So to prohibit work on human embryonic stem cells will thus do severe collateral damage to the new and exciting research on iPS cells."[33]

> "Human embryonic stem cells remain the gold standard for pluripotency. So to prohibit work on human embryonic stem cells will thus do severe collateral damage to the new and exciting research on iPS cells."[33]
>
> —Francis S. Collins, the director of the NIH.

"A Vital Research Tool"

Besides being the gold standard for comparison purposes, embryonic stem cells—not iPS cells—remain the only window scientists have to study exactly how humans develop at the earliest stages of life. "There is still much to be learned about human [ES] cells, and about how stem cells derive from human embryos," argues stem cell researcher George Q. Daley. "When we still have so much to learn, how can we conclude that [ES] cells are no longer needed?"[34]

Daley and other scientists recognize that advances in different sorts of stem cell research do not necessarily mean that other kinds of research are obsolete or unnecessary. Breakthroughs in making iPS cells do not necessarily represent a defeat for ESC research. Rather, these different branches of stem cell research should be seen as complementary. Scientists should retain all tools at their disposal for stem cell research. "No matter how much progress is made with other forms of stem cells," Daley concludes, "Embryonic stem cells will remain a vital research tool and any expulsion of [ES] cells from the researcher's toolkit would greatly weaken stem cell research overall."[35]

Chapter Three

Should the Federal Government Fund Embryonic Stem Cell Research?

The Federal Government Should Fund Embryonic Stem Cell Research

- Only the federal government has the resources to adequately support basic research into stem cells.
- Bush-era funding limits hampered scientific research and careers.
- Government funding assures consistent and ethical regulation of stem cell research.

The Debate at a Glance

The Federal Government Should Not Fund Embryonic Stem Cell Research

- Taxpayer money should not be used for morally controversial experiments.
- Government funding of science is often inefficient and wasteful.
- Government funding of embryonic stem cell research may violate federal law.

The Federal Government Should Fund Embryonic Stem Cell Research

"Human embryonic stem cell research . . . has the potential to facilitate development of new and better therapies and potential cures for some of mankind's most devastating diseases. As a result, we believe that federal funding of human embryonic stem cell research should be allowed to resume."

—John R. Layton, the president of the Boston Biomedical Research Institute board of trustees.

Quoted in *Tech*, "New Twist in Stem Cell Lawsuit," November 23, 2010. http://tech.mit.edu.

Consider these questions as you read:

1. What advantages does public funding have over private funding of scientific research? Which do you believe is most important?
2. Why might government funding restrictions have special relevance for scientists at the early stages of their careers?
3. How does government funding influence the ethics of stem cell research, and are there other ways to achieve this outcome?

Editor's note: The discussion that follows presents common arguments made in support of this perspective, reinforced by facts, quotes, and examples taken from various sources.

For most of the first decade of this century, the federal government placed significant restrictions on its funding of human embryonic stem cell research. In 2001 President George W. Bush issued an executive order that allowed for funding of research on already existing ESC lines but banned funding for research on lines created after that time. As a result of this policy, scientists had only twenty-one viable ESC lines for research. The policy remained in effect until 2009, when President Barack Obama issued his own executive order that ended Bush's ban. By October 2012 the NIH had established new guidelines and had approved more than 170 human ESC lines for government-funded research projects.

Obama's decision to reverse Bush's executive order showed the folly of limits on government funding for stem cell research. The federally imposed restrictions had held back the American scientific community—even as foreign researchers moved ahead—and prevented the potential benefits of research from being realized.

Essential Funding for Basic Research

Government funding is essential for research. The NIH, with an annual budget of more than $30 billion, accounts for more than a third of the total money America spends on medical research. NIH grants are especially important for supporting basic research that expands knowledge but has no immediate or obvious application or product. Human ESC research, which dates only to 1998, still mostly falls in the basic research category.

Many private grants focus more on applied research than basic research because private investors want to make money from their investments, and donors like seeing the practical effects of their donations. As a result, these grants usually go to projects that have a high likelihood of developing a specific (and patentable) new treatment, drug, or procedure. Embryonic stem cell research has not yet reached this point. For this reason, private funding of ESC research can fill in only some of the gap created if federal government funding is restricted. But another reason is a matter of simple numbers. The NIH spends $900 million on stem cell research every year—an amount that private donors simply cannot match year in and year out. Indeed, the focus of many philanthropic grants is to help researchers get to the point where they can compete for federal dollars and the sustained funding government dollars provide.

How Spending Limits Hamper Scientific Inquiry

When Bush announced limits on federal funding of human ESC research in 2001, his decision had damaging ripple effects in the scientific community. Some stem cell scientists contemplated leaving for other countries. A notable example of a person who did leave was Roger Pederson, a biomedical researcher at the University of California at San Francisco who left in 2001 to head a stem cell research institute in England. His story is indicative of the reality that "a loss of federal funding threatens American competitiveness in stem cell research,"[36] in the words of stem cell scientist George Q. Daley.

A more recent example of how funding restrictions affect scientific careers is Candace Kerr, a stem cell scientist at Johns Hopkins University in Maryland. Following Obama's reversal of Bush's policy, she had successfully gotten an NIH grant for embryonic stem cell research. But in August 2010 her project was shut down because of a judge's ruling in a lawsuit seeking a halt to all US government funding of such research. The ruling was later reversed, but Kerr has decided to abandon embryonic stem cell research anyway. "The shock of what happened last year, coming out of nowhere, makes us really skeptical about moving forward,"[37] she said in 2011.

> "A loss of federal funding threatens American competitiveness in stem cell research."[36]
>
> —George Q. Daley, a medical professor at Harvard University and the director of the Stem Cell Transplantation Program at Children's Hospital Boston.

Kerr's circumstances are shared by many. Most of the research funded by NIH grants is performed by graduate students and postdoctoral researchers who are at a critical point in their careers in which they must decide what research to pursue and in what field to specialize. Many of them rely on government research grants to cover their living expenses. According to the Stem Cell Action Coalition, banning or limiting federal funding would mean that students doing embryonic stem cell research would "be financially forced to prematurely exit their programs and are at *significant risk of losing their research careers entirely.*"[38]

Harming Scientific Collaboration

Federal government restrictions have other negative effects, even for ESC researchers who successfully get private funding for their work.

One is professional isolation. Scientists typically rely on collaboration with other scientists—the free sharing of information and experimental results—to advance their field. However, government rules limiting funding for certain types of research create obstacles to such communication. Under President Bush's stem cell directive, for example, researchers frequently ran up against rules banning communication with colleagues or projects that did receive federal funds. "You had . . . young researchers in a lab next door who could benefit by learning what is going on," said stem cell research activist Amy Comstock Rick, "but they can't if they're on federal training grants. . . . It's been holding science back."[39]

In addition, scientists receiving funds from private sources are often bound by contractual agreements not to share their results. Corporations funding research want to be able to patent or otherwise exploit whatever usable information is found. Private funding, argues stem cell scientist Lawrence S.B. Goldstein, thereby creates "inherent conflicts between the companies' natural tendency to keep their activities secret (so as not to tip off the competition) and academia's tradition of sharing research results with the scientific community and the general public."[40] Ensuring federal funding of embryonic stem cell research gives scientists an alternative to relying on private sources and the strings that are often attached.

The Dickey-Wicker Amendment

Some opponents of embryonic stem cell research funding have claimed that it violates federal law. They cite the Dickey-Wicker Amendment, a provision first attached to the 1996 NIH budget (and reauthorized ever since) that states no federal funds can pay for experiments in which human embryos are created or destroyed for research purposes. The amendment, which predates human ESC research by two years, clearly prohibits the deliberate destruction of embryos. But it does not ban research on human cells derived from human embryos.

The NIH interprets Dickey-Wicker to mean that federal funds cannot be used for the creation of ESC lines but that federal funds can

Many Americans Support Government Funding of Embryonic Stem Cell Research

According to a national online 2012 poll of 1,052 likely US voters, most say they favor—either strongly or somewhat—government support of human embryonic stem cell research. The poll was commissioned by Research! America, a nonprofit public education and advocacy alliance concerned with healthcare.

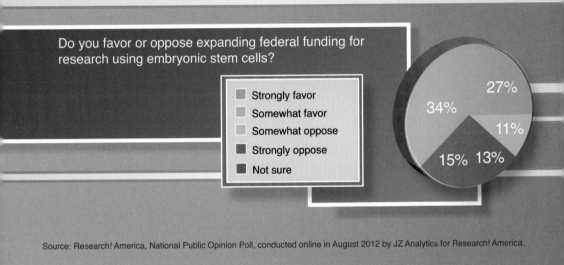

Do you favor or oppose expanding federal funding for research using embryonic stem cells?

- Strongly favor
- Somewhat favor
- Somewhat oppose
- Strongly oppose
- Not sure

27%
34%
11%
15% 13%

Source: Research! America, National Public Opinion Poll, conducted online in August 2012 by JZ Analytics for Research! America.

be used to research ESCs themselves. In 2013 a federal appeals court rejected a legal challenge to federal government funding, affirming the NIH's interpretation of the Dickey-Wicker rule.

Government Funding Ensures Ethical Research

Opponents of human ESC research often cite ethical objections, but the truth is that federal funding of such research helps ensure that it is performed ethically. Under Bush, there was no federal oversight or role for prescribing standards for privately funded programs that procured embryos and created stem cell lines. When President Obama issued his own executive order authorizing funding of ESC research, he also ordered the NIH to develop and standardize proper procedures for the procurement of stem cells.

The NIH published its guidelines in July 2009. These guidelines restrict federal funding to cell lines derived from leftover embryos that were created for reproductive purposes at fertility clinics. They require that the donors (the clients of the clinics) give voluntary written consent for their excess embryos to be used for research. "With expanded funding comes expanded oversight," writes bioethics professor Robert Streiffer, "and with expanded oversight comes the ability to set and enforce ethical standards."[41] Improved oversight and ethical standards is another reason for supporting federal funding of this important and promising branch of biomedical research.

> "With expanded funding comes expanded oversight, and with expanded oversight comes the ability to set and enforce ethical standards."[41]
>
> —Robert Streiffer, a professor of bioethics and philosophy at the University of Wiscsonsin at Madison.

The Federal Government Should Not Fund Embryonic Stem Cell Research

"Americans should not be forced to pay for experiments that destroy human life, have produced no real-world treatments, and violate federal law."

—Steven H. Aden, senior counsel for the Alliance Defending Freedom, an organization of conservative christian lawyers and activists.

Quoted in Alliance Defending Freedom, "*Sherley v. Sebelius* Resource Page: Needless, Illegal Taxpayer Funding of Embryo-Destructive Research Stands," January 7, 2013. www.alliancedefendingfreedom.org.

Consider these questions as you read:

1. Do you believe the question of whether to fund ESC research is a question that can be settled or informed by public opinion polls? Why or why not?
2. What can Congress do to clarify whether funding embryonic stem cell research violates US law? Explain.
3. What analogy is made between stem cell research and IVF research? Do you believe the analogy is an effective argument against government funding for stem cell research?

Editor's note: The discussion that follows presents common arguments made in support of this perspective, reinforced by facts, quotes, and examples taken from various sources.

James A. Thomson's 1998 experiments that resulted in creating the first human ESC lines were done with zero government funding. But ever since then, scientists, politicians, and the public have wrangled over whether the federal government should fund ESC experiments. When President George W. Bush placed restrictions on ESC funding in 2001, stem cell proponents appealed to public opinion by offering glittering prospects of miracle cures and treatments. These arguments succeeded in persuading some states (such as California) to fund such research on their own and contributed to President Barack Obama's decision to reverse Bush's restrictions in 2009. But embryonic stem cells have failed to deliver on the promises of their advocates. There remain compelling ethical, practical, and legal arguments why the government should not fund human ESC research.

Ethical Objections

The central objection to ESC research is simple: this research requires the destruction of human embryos. For many, this is an unacceptable destruction of innocent human life. Government funding compounds this ethical offense by creating financial incentives to kill embryos or to create embryos for the purpose of destroying them. In his 2001 executive order, President Bush sought to limit federal funding of human ESC research to preexisting lines rather than contribute to further embryo killing. As he stated in 2007 when vetoing legislation that funded ESC research, such funding crossed a "moral line" by compelling taxpayers "for the first time in our history to support the deliberate destruction of human embryos."[42]

Views on the moral status of early-stage embryos and whether their preservation justifies a cessation of stem cell research are still debated. What is beyond debate, however, is that a consensus does not exist on this morally divisive issue. Even if a majority of people support stem cell research, those who do not should not be forced to pay tax dollars for research they passionately oppose on ethical grounds. The American public recognizes this; an August 27, 2010, Rasmussen poll found that 57 percent of those polled oppose all federal funding for research that destroys human embryos, and only 33 percent indicated support.

The Dickey-Wicker Amendment

Federal funding of human ESC research is not only immoral and impractical but also appears to violate federal law. In 1996 Republican representatives Jay Dickey and Roger Wicker attached an amendment to the

Many Americans Oppose Government Funding of Embryonic Stem Cell Research

In 2010 the United States Conference of Catholic Bishops (USCCB) commissioned a poll on public attitudes on human embyonic stem cell research. Two of the poll's questions focused on govenment funding for such work. The USCCB, part of the Roman Catholic church, actively opposes embryonic stem cell research.

Stem cells are the basic cells from which all of a person's tissues and organs develop. Congress is considering the question of federal funding for experiments using stem cells from human embryos. The live embryos would be destroyed in their first week of development to obtain these cells. Do you support or oppose using your federal tax dollars for such experiments?

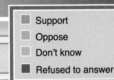

- ☐ Support
- ☐ Oppose
- ☐ Don't know
- ☐ Refused to answer

38%

47%

11%

3%

Stem cells can be obtained by destroying human embryos. They can also be obtained from adults, from placentas left over from live births, and in other ways that do no harm to the donor. Scientists disagree on which source may end up being most successful in treating diseases. How would you prefer your tax dollars to be used this year for stem cell research?

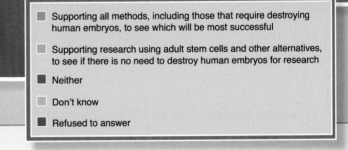

21%

57%

9%

10%

3%

- ☐ Supporting all methods, including those that require destroying human embryos, to see which will be most successful
- ☐ Supporting research using adult stem cells and other alternatives, to see if there is no need to destroy human embryos for research
- ☐ Neither
- ☐ Don't know
- ☐ Refused to answer

Note: Figures may not total 100 percent due to rounding.

Source: ICR/Internation Communications Research, "Stem Cell Research Study," September 8–14, 2010. http://old.usccb.org.com.

budget of the NIH. The Dickey-Wicker Amendment prohibits federal funds for any "research in which a human embryo or embryos are destroyed."[43] It has been reaffirmed by Congress in subsequent years to the present day.

Human ESC research involves the destruction of embryos to harvest the cells. In 1999 officials at the NIH sought to sidestep this clear prohibition. They argued that federal funds could not pay for the creation of ESCs (by destroying embryos), but the government could still pay for research using ESCs created using nongovernment funds. Such an interpretation goes against common sense. If embryonic stem cell research requires stem cell lines, and creation of these lines requires the destruction of embryos, than all ESC research is entangled in embryo destruction. As such, it should not be eligible for federal funding under the Dickey-Wicker Amendment. In 2010 Wicker, now a US senator, said during Senate testimony that he believed the amendment he coauthored means that "the Federal Government should not be involved in this controversial life-altering research with taxpayer dollars."[44]

> "The Federal Government should not be involved in this controversial life-altering research with taxpayer dollars."[44]
>
> —Roger Wicker, a US senator from Mississippi and the coauthor of the Dickey-Wicker Amendment.

Unfortunately, in the case of *Sherley v. Sebelius* in January 2013, the courts ultimately deferred to the original NIH interpretation that ESC derivation and research could be separated. Congress should revisit the issue and amend the law's language to clarify that its prohibitions apply to ESC research.

Funding Should Go to Other Forms of Stem Cell Research

The federal government can support stem cell research in many other ways. One would be to increase funding for projects involving adult stem cells. Adult stem cells obtained from bone marrow have already been used successfully to treat leukemia and other blood disorders. Likewise, stem cells obtained from fatty tissue and other parts of the body are being test-ed in the fight against diabetes, heart disease, and other conditions. Adult stem cells are superior to ESCs both ethically (no embryos need to be destroyed) and practically (they do not have the rejection by the body or tumor problems of ESCs). James Sherley, a researcher who works with adult stem cells (and a plaintiff in *Sherley v. Sebelius*) argues that abandoning research on ESCs does not mean the elimination of all stem cell research. Government funding should instead be directed at alternatives such as adult stem cells that are, Sherley says, "the biologically superior choice for developing new treatment strategies, because adult stem cells are the natural cells for repair and renewal of injured and diseased tissue."[45]

Human iPS cells also offer a worthwhile alternative for federal funding. These cells are adult cells that have most of the valuable properties of embryonic stem cells but, like other types of adult cells, avoid the embryo destruction and foreign rejection problems of ESCs. These "other lines of inquiry are unquestionably far more promising than ES cells," writes journalist Michael Fumento. However, because scientists are competing for more government money than is available, Fumento writes, "a dime spent on dead-end ES work is a dime unavailable for research, stem cell or otherwise, with true promise to heal the sick."[46]

Government Funding Is Not Necessary for Scientific Progress

The government is not the only source of funds for scientists seeking to research human ESCs. Private companies, charitable foundations, and individual donors have pumped hundreds of millions, if not billions, of dollars into this research. The potential benefits that embryonic stem cell proponents love to cite—new cures and treatments for disease—are powerful inducements for charitable foundations and possibly even more appealing to private companies seeking blockbuster new medicines and products. Indeed, nongovernmental sources have given hundreds of millions of dollars to ESC research. According to analysts Sigrid Fry-Revere and Molly Elgin, "There is little risk that stem cell research will go unfunded."[47]

Fry-Revere and Elgin argue that the current debate over government funding of ESC research recalls the debates of the 1970s over assisted reproduction and IVF research. "Advocates insisted that [government] funding [of] IVF research was crucial for the United States to maintain its position as a leader in reproductive medicine," they note. The proponents of government funding lost that debate, but their failure did not stop America from becoming a global leader in this field, thanks to private investment. "Today in the United States," write Fry-Revere and Elgin, "IVF for humans is estimated as a $3 billion dollar a year industry—all of it developed without any government funding." Likewise, they argue that the best way to make progress and assure US supremacy in ESC research is "to allow the private sector to grow, unimpeded by cumbersome regulation and political controversy."[48]

> "A dime spent on dead-end ES work is a dime unavailable for research, stem cell or otherwise, with true promise to heal the sick."[46]
>
> —Michael Fumento, a science journalist and the author of *Bioevolution: How Biotechnology Is Changing Our World.*

Scientific Progress and Respect for Human Life

Even those who support embryonic stem cell research recognize its ethical and practical limitations. President Bill Clinton's National Bioethics Advisory Commission in 1999 gave a green light to such research but acknowledged that "human embryos deserve respect as a form of human life" and that destroying embryos "is justifiable only if no less morally problematic alternatives are available for advancing the research."[49] With the rapid development of adult stem cell treatment and the discovery and improvements of human iPS cells, an honest appraisal would lead one to conclude that there are indeed "less morally problematic alternatives" available for scientists and patients hoping for cures for disease. It is time to stop the federal funding of human ESC research.

Chapter Four

Are More Government Regulations Needed for Stem Cell Research?

Onerous Government Regulations Are Hampering Progress in Stem Cell Research

- The United States is falling behind other countries in stem cell treatments because of government rules and regulations.
- Stem cells from a person's own body should not be classified as a drug that requires FDA regulation.
- People should have the right to pursue their own medical treatments.

The Debate at a Glance

The Government Should Carefully Regulate Stem Cell Research and Treatments

- Numerous clinics have offered stem cell treatments without appropriate clinical trials or proof of efficacy.
- Patients and their families are being victimized by unscrupulous stem cell treatment providers.
- The FDA should have regulatory authority over stem cells cultured and reintroduced into patients to ensure that people are not victimized by unsafe and/or ineffective treatments.

Onerous Government Regulations Are Hampering Progress in Stem Cell Research

"There is no readily identifiable public health risk rationale for FDA's current regulatory posture regarding therapy employing adult autologous [from the patient's own tissues] stem cells."

—Christopher J. Centeno, physician, and Stephen Faulkner, an employee of the Centeno-Schultz Clinic, a provider of certain stem cell therapies.

Christopher J. Centeno and Stephen Faulkner, "The Use of Mesenchymal Stem Cells in Orthopedics: Review of the Literature, Current Research, the Regulatory Landscape," *Journal of American Physicians and Surgeons,* Summer 2011, p. 43.

Consider these questions as you read:

1. What role should government play in overseeing new medicines and treatments? Explain your answer.
2. Do you believe one's own stem cells should be considered a drug under federal law? Why or why not?
3. Many advocates of less regulation are stem cell entrepreneurs. How should their views be taken?

Editor's note: The discussion that follows presents common arguments made in support of this perspective, reinforced by facts, quotes, and examples taken from various sources.

Bartolo Colón was a pretty good Major League Baseball pitcher whose career seemed to be over in 2009 because of a series of injuries to his pitching arm, including a torn rotator cuff in his shoulder. In April 2010, in Colón's native Dominican Republic, Dr. Joseph Purita extracted Colón's stem cells from his bone marrow and fatty tissue and injected them into his elbow and shoulder. The procedure apparently helped Colón; the thirty-eight-year-old subsequently made a successful comeback with the New York Yankees in 2011, throwing the ball as fast as he did when he was younger. "What changed?" asked science journalist Ferris Jabr, who then answered his own question: "It seems that Colón has grown a new tendon thanks to stem cell therapy."[50]

Michael Phelan, a software executive, is another patient who has sought stem cell treatment. He has multiple sclerosis (MS), a disease that affects the nervous system. Conventional drugs and treatment were ineffective, so he traveled to a clinic in Panama to have adult stem cells generated from his body fat and then injected back into his body. The stem cells cured the vision and urinary problems associated with MS, he said in a 2013 interview. In addition, he explained that his "mental and physical energy improved dramatically. . . . I had reduced spasticity, less headaches and improved balance."[51]

Promising Treatments Are Delayed

The cases of Colón and Phelan are examples of the huge potential of adult stem cells to rejuvenate the body, reverse aging, and treat diseases. The promise of adult stem cell treatments has attracted tens of thousands of patients to try them. However, like Colón and Phelan, most patients must travel outside the United States to actually receive treatment. The US government—specifically the FDA—is partly to blame for this, according to some stem cell research advocates. Much of their criticism is directed at the FDA's requirement that stem cells be subject to expensive and time-consuming human clinical trials before they can be approved for use as medicine.

Adult stem cells, which exist in various regions of the body, can help the body recover from injury or illness by dividing into progeny of different types. Hematopoietic stem cells, found in bone marrow, can produce all types of blood cells. Mesenchymal stem cells, also found in bone marrow as well as in fat and muscle, give rise to cells that form bones, fat, and the connective tissue found in tendons. Neural stem cells, found in brain tissue, can produce neurons and other types of cells found in the brain. Stem cells work naturally as healers and repairers of the body; the theory is that when cultivated outside the body and injected, they could fix damaged tissue.

Adult stem cells have been caught up in the controversy over human ESC research. But unlike ESC cells, no embryos are destroyed since adult cells can be harvested from the adult body or from umbilical cord blood. Adult stem cells also make possible autologous medical treatments—treatments in which the patient's own tissues are used to harvest stem cells. This makes possible personalized medical treatments that avoid the body's immune response.

Drug or Medical Procedure?

FDA regulations designed for drugs are of questionable worth when applied to autologous stem cell treatments, which are very individualized. Stem cell clinics are not factories that manufacture pills. They are more analogous to fertility clinics that take the sperm and eggs of patients, do some manipulation in the lab, and reimplant them in the patient (in this case, the female's uterus). IVF clinics are providing a service, not a drug, and are not regulated by the FDA or the federal government. Stem cell clinics do something similar: they harvest cells, cultivate them, and reintroduce them to the patient. For these reasons, stem cell research should operate under similar levels of government regulation.

Christopher J. Centeno, the director of Regenerative Science, a stem cell clinic that has been the target of FDA investigations, says people should have the right to decide their own medical care and what to do with their own cells and tissues: "If a loved one is dying in intensive care and a well-done study shows that the patient's own cells can be used to help, does the patient get to decide to use those cells, or is that a decision for the FDA? Will the patient still be alive while we wait on Washington to issue this decision?"[52]

Waiting for FDA Approval Could Be Fatal

Keith Lockitch, a doctor and writer from the Ayn Rand Center for Individual Rights, argues that the FDA has a record of denying drugs and treatments to patients while they are undergoing government review. The cost of getting a new drug developed, studied, and approved can reach $1 billion. The process may take years, during which the drugs are unavailable for patients not accepted into clinical studies. Many drugs never make it to market because the cost of seeking FDA approval is too high. Allowing the FDA to treat stem cells as a drug may hamper stem cell treatments the same way. "How many promising avenues of adult stem cell research will be cut off by the same regulatory oversight?" asks Lockitch. "And how many of us who could benefit from new treatments will instead be forced to endure pain and debilitating disease?"[53]

Using autologous stem cells means that each patient is getting their own stem cells back. This makes it difficult for stem cell treatment providers to "run a large-scale, randomized drug trial and ensure consistency from one use of a drug to another," argues former FDA officials Scott Gottlieb and Coleen Klasmeier. "The FDA requirements, designed for products manufactured and sold on a mass scale, can't be readily satisfied when it comes to treatments that are personalized to individual patients."[54]

The result, according to Gottlieb and Klasmeier, is that "most of the science of using adult stem cells for regenerative medicine is unfolding in Britain, Singapore and Israel precisely because of the FDA's bent to hold with misgiving anything novel in medicine."[55]

> "Most of the science of using adult stem cells for regenerative medicine is unfolding in Britain, Singapore and Israel precisely because of the FDA's bent to hold with misgiving anything novel in medicine."[55]
>
> —Scott Gottlieb and Coleen Klasmeier, former officials with the FDA who later left government to work with private companies developing cell-based therapies.

Are Animals Better Off than People?

In examining whether overly stringent regulations are hampering stem cell research and treatment options, one interesting comparison is to look at stem cell treatments for animals. The hurdles created by the FDA, such as requirements for clinical studies, do not apply to animals. An ironic consequence of the absence of these regulatory hurdles is that stem cell treatments for animals have blossomed in the United States

Some Regulations Have Questionable Value

Opponents of strict FDA regulatory policies note that stem cells taken from a patient's own body are safer than other types of stem cells. Other cells introduce more foreign and unpredictable elements and may cause unwanted tumors and/or reactions from the body's immune system. The group Patients for Stem Cells asserts that the FDA should not have the power to regulate or ban patients from using their own stem cells.

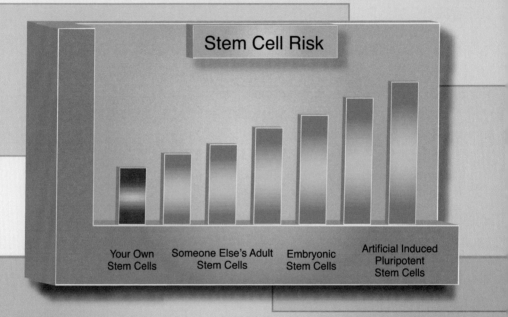

Stem Cell Risk

Your Own Stem Cells | Someone Else's Adult Stem Cells | Embryonic Stem Cells | Artificial Induced Pluripotent Stem Cells

Source: Patients For Stem Cells, "How Safe Are Stem Cells?," 2012. www.patientsforstemcells.org.

even as human treatments have languished. Journalist David Cyranoski estimates that thousands of animals have been beneficiaries of stem cell research. One company alone, "Vet-Stem, a company based in Poway, California, has provided stem-cell treatments to more than 5,000 horses, 4,300 dogs and 120 cats since treating its first patient in 2004."[56]

Other private companies, university veterinary departments, and individual veterinarians have also provided stem cell treatments. The procedure is basically the same as what was done to Colón and Phelan: fat or bone marrow cells are extracted, and then stem cells are cultured, concentrated, and injected into the affected area. Animals have seen dramatic improvements in joint stiffness, mobility, and even skin conditions. "We can do things sooner for our patients without 10 years of expensive clinical trials,"[57] notes Shila Nordone of the American Kennel Association Canine Health Foundation.

Extend Stem Cell Research Benefits to All

The potential benefits that adult stem cell treatments bring to these animals and to individuals such as Colón and Phelan should not be denied to others because of onerous FDA drug testing requirements and other government regulations. "I'm grateful to have access to treatment," said Phelan, reflecting on how stem cells helped his condition with MS. "But it should be available to everyone. . . . America should be fast tracking this treatment, not slowing the adoption process to the crawl involved in drug approval." Failure to streamline the adoption process, he argues, is "a crime against ill people who can't afford to travel overseas for treatment."[58]

"America should be fast tracking this treatment, not slowing the adoption process to the crawl involved in drug approval."[58]

—Michael Phelan, a software company executive who traveled to Panama to receive stem cell treatment for multiple sclerosis.

The Government Should Carefully Regulate Stem Cell Research and Treatments

"My main desire is to see stem cells introduced into the clinic only via responsible, rigorous and ethical scientific testing. To ensure that this happens, there is a clear need for strong, clear and independently enforced regulations."

—Douglas Sipp, author of the *Stem Cell Treatment Monitor Blog.*

Quoted in Paul Knoepfler, "Interviews with Centeno and Sipp on Key Case on FDA Authority over Stem Cells," *Knoepfler Lab Stem Cell Blog,* 2012. www.ipscell.com.

Consider these questions as you read:

1. What role should the federal government play in protecting people from potentially unsafe treatments and from people who make false promises about those treatments?
2. Do you believe new stem cell treatments should get the same amount of government scrutiny as new drugs? Why or why not?
3. If you had the money and a disease that was not treatable by available methods, would you travel to another country and try a stem cell treatment? Why or why not?

Editor's note: The discussion that follows presents common arguments made in support of this perspective, reinforced by facts, quotes, and examples taken from various sources.

Adam Susser has cerebral palsy. His brain was deprived of oxygen when he was born in 2001, leaving him unable to control motor functions or to see. In 2004 and 2005 his parents, Gary and Judy Susser, took him to Tijuana, Mexico, where Adam received multiple injections of stem cells (from umbilical cord blood) at a cost of $25,000. Their hope was that the stem cells—precursor cells that have the potential to develop into other types of cells—could somehow repair or restore the damaged tissue in Adam's brain and nervous system. By 2013, after seeing no improvement in Adam's condition, their hopes had faded. "While they are advocates of 'responsible' stem cell research," writes Florida reporter Marcia Heroux Pounds, "they warn other parents against making trips to Costa Rica, Mexico, Russia, or other offshore clinics for experimental treatments."[59]

Hype Versus Reality

Stem cell research stands at a pivotal point in its development. Scientists and others seeking government and private research funding for stem cell research have for many years emphasized the potential of stem cells to reverse the aging process or treat heretofore untreatable diseases. Clinics both in the United States and abroad have advertised various stem cell treatments, including some in which a person's own stem cells from bone marrow or fatty tissue are extracted, purified and cultured, and placed back in the patient.

However, the reality of adult stem cell treatments has fallen short of these stoked expectations. As of 2013 the FDA had officially approved only one stem cell product. That product, Hemacord, is derived from umbilical cord blood and is used to help people with metabolic and other disorders that affect their ability to produce their own blood cells. Aside from Hemacord, most of the recognized adult stem cell treatments are otherwise known as bone marrow transplants. During these procedures bone marrow—now known to be a source of stem cells—is transplanted from a donor to treat a limited range of diseases affecting the blood and the immune systems.

Online Scams

The paucity of established stem cell treatments has not stopped desperate patients and their families from looking at stem cells as a possible answer to their prayers. Nor has it stopped clinics and individuals from offering stem cell therapies and treatments. In 2012 journalist Scott Pelley presented a *60 Minutes* investigation into stem cell treatments, noting that patients searching for solutions to their medical problems can find "hundreds of credible-looking websites offering stem cell cures in overseas clinics."[60] But behind these online promises lies a shadowy group of unregulated and sometimes unethical operators.

Pelley investigated Stem Tech Labs, an Ecuador-based clinic that promised "modern day medical miracle" cures for seventy diseases. Pelley worked in cooperation with Gary and Judy Susser. After the Sussers talked on the phone with the clinic founder, Alabama physician Dan Eckland, they paid $5,000 for a shipment of stem cells to be sent to their home. The Sussers and *60 Minutes* had the shipment sent for analysis to federal researchers at Duke University. When they analyzed the shipment, the researchers found the stem cells to be dead and disintegrating and riddled with cellular debris. Joanne Kurtzburg, the chief scientific officer of Duke University's stem cell research program, told Pelley that injecting the dead cells into one's blood or spinal fluid could cause stroke and other dangerous or even fatal reactions.

Serious Risks

The risks of stem cell treatments gone wrong are real. In 2013 the state of Florida suspended the license of Dr. Zannos Grekos after two patients receiving stem cell injections died under his care. Stem cells have powers that make them potentially more dangerous than chemical drugs. Cells may multiply, migrate to different parts of the body, or form tumors. Stem cells derived from fat or bone marrow may not function properly when placed in the bloodstream, muscles, or brain.

Like Stem Tech Labs and other stem cell practitioners, Grekos had a website in which he minimized these risks while promoting stem cells as helpful for numerous conditions. However, there is no established scientific evidence that stem cell treatments can treat cerebral palsy, multiple sclerosis, ALS, or other diseases often mentioned by these clinics. "Stem cell therapies that purport to treat everything from shot knees and slipped disks to autism, multiple sclerosis, and Parkinson's disease are rightly regarded as modern-day quackery," writes science journalist Gergana Koleva. "That is because unscrupulous doctors have seized on the promise of this exciting new science and used it to peddle unproven treatments to desperate and ill-informed patients."[61]

The Importance of FDA Regulation

Grekos and Eckland may be extreme examples and not necessarily representative of all scientists and doctors offering stem cell treatment. However, they do serve as a powerful reminder of why strict government regulation of stem cell research and treatments are needed. In the United States, the FDA is the government agency responsible for ensuring that medicines are safe and effective and that they work as promised.

The FDA thus has both the authority and obligation to ensure that stem cell treatments are safe and effective for their intended use. To fulfill this obligation, the FDA periodically inspects facilities that manufacture stem cells for reinjection. It requires adequate safeguards to ensure the safety, purity, and potency of products used in treatments for ill patients. It requires data from animal studies to aid in evaluating risks. Finally, it requires a critical mass of well-designed human clinical trials for stem cell treatments to receive FDA approval and be prescribed for patients. These include double-blind experiments that compare patients receiving stem cell treatments with those who receive a placebo, or inactive substance, instead.

> "Stem cell therapies that purport to treat everything from shot knees and slipped disks to autism, multiple sclerosis, and Parkinson's disease are rightly regarded as modern-day quackery."[61]
>
> —Gergana Koleva writes about health issues and consumer fraud for *Forbes*.

Some stem cell treatment providers claim that they should not be subject to these strict FDA rules because they are using autologous methods—that is, the treatments patients receive consist of their own extracted stem cells. They contend that a person should be able to decide whether to use his or her own cells without government interference. Additionally, these treatment providers argue that they are not making drugs. Rather, they are performing a medical procedure, which

Government Regulations Have Not Hurt Efforts to Develop Treatments

The number of stem cell clinical trials that have registered with the National Institutes of Health database at Clinicaltrials.gov has grown steadily between 2001 and 2011. Clinical trials are a necessary step in developing medical treatments. The steady rise in clinical trials suggests that US government regulations are working and have not stifled stem cell research.

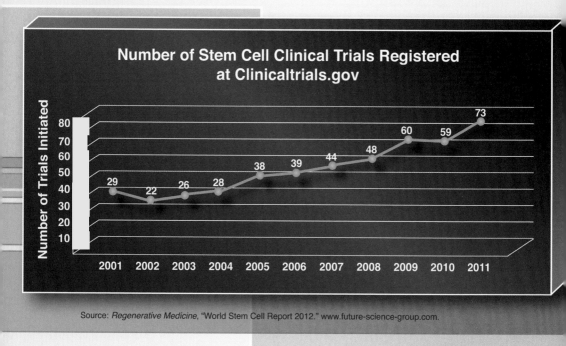

Number of Stem Cell Clinical Trials Registered at Clinicaltrials.gov

Source: *Regenerative Medicine*, "World Stem Cell Report 2012." www.future-science-group.com.

generally does not come under FDA scrutiny. But the FDA has determined that stem cell treatments involve more than simply extracting and reinjecting cells. The labs process the bone marrow or fatty tissue taken from the patient to isolate the stem cells in that tissue and then return only the cultivated stem cells (usually in a different part of the body from where they were first extracted). Such a procedure, the FDA has determined, constitutes the "manufacture, holding for sale, and distribution of an unapproved biological drug product."[62]

In July 2012 the US District Court in Washington, DC, agreed with the FDA and affirmed the agency's right to regulate stem cell therapies. "It is much too simplistic to think that stem cells are removed from the body and then returned to the body without a 'manufacturing process' that includes the risk of transmission of communicable diseases," says bioethicist Leigh Turner. "Maintaining the FDA's role as watchdog and regulatory authority is imperative."[63]

Regulation Does Not Hamper Stem Cell Research

The FDA process is working. As of 2013 there were more than 3,500 clinical studies of stem cell treatments worldwide being monitored by the FDA, indicating a thriving research scene. A robust regulatory structure is not only important for consumers but also for stem cell researchers and companies. Robin L. Smith, chief executive officer of NeoStem, a biotechnology firm focusing on stem cells and cellular therapy, argues that government regulations, "instead of squelching innovation

> "Maintaining the FDA's role as watchdog and regulatory authority is imperative."[63]
>
> —Leigh Turner, a professor of bioethics at the University of Minnesota.

. . . [can] provide consistency and predictability for medical product developers."[64] Regulation can prevent gross abuses or deaths from stem cells that may taint public perception of stem cells and retard the field's development. Although the delays created by these rules may be frustrating to people who are ill or caring for ill family members, in the long run they provide the best hope that stem cell research may someday help them and others like them.

Source Notes

Overview: Stem Cell Research

1. Quoted in *USA Today,* "Gurdon, Yamanaka Win Nobel Prize in Medicine," October 8, 2012. www.usatoday.com.
2. National Institutes of Health, "Stem Cell Information: Stem Cell Basics." http://stemcells.nih.gov.

Chapter One: Is Embryonic Stem Cell Research Ethical?

3. Joseph Panno, *Stem Cell Research: Medical Applications and Ethical Controversy.* New York: Facts On File, 2005, p. 72.
4. Panno, *Stem Cell Research*, p. 72.
5. John Yockey, "Does the End Justify the Means?," *Catholic Herald News,* June 9, 2011. www.chnonline.org.
6. Quotcd in Cheryl Wetzstein, "Obama Defunds 'Snowflake Babies,'" *Washington Times,* March 4, 2012. www.washingtontimes.com.
7. George W. Bush, *Decision Points.* New York: Random House, 2010, p. 112.
8. Justin D. Barnard, "The Embryo Troubles of Obama's Top Doctor," *Public Discourse,* July 13, 2009. www.thepublicdiscourse.com.
9. Quoted in Gina Kolata, "Man Who Helped Start Stem Cell War May End It," *New York Times*, November 22, 2007. www.nytimes.com.
10. National Institutes of Health, "National Institutes of Health Guidelines on Human Stem Cell Research," NIH, 2009. http://stemcells.nih.gov.
11. Insoo Hyan, "Stem Cells," in *From Birth to Death and Bench to Clinic: The Hastings Center Bioethics Briefing Book for Journalists, Policymakers and Campaigns,* ed. Mary Crowley. Garrison, NY: Hastings Center, 2008, p. 161.
12. Lawrence S.B. Goldstein and Meg Schneider, *Stem Cells for Dummies.* Hoboken, NJ: Wiley, 2010, p. 287.

13. Quoted in Goldstein and Schneider, *Stem Cells for Dummies,* p. 241.

14. Quoted in Boston Children's Hospital Staff, "Stem Cell Research: A Father's Story," *Thriving* (blog), July 7, 2009. http://childrenshospital blog.org.

15. Quoted in Boston Children's Hospital Staff, "Stem Cell Research."

16. Quoted in Boston Children's Hospital Staff, "Stem Cell Research."

17. Quoted in Boston Children's Hospital Staff, "Stem Cell Research."

Chapter Two: Is Embryonic Stem Cell Research Still Necessary?

18. Andy Lewis, "Induced Pluripotent Stem Cells: An Amazing Breakthrough in the Stem Cell Debate," Ethics and Religious Liberty Commission, January 14, 2008. www.erlc.com.

19. David van Gend, "An Obituary for Human Cloning," *AFA Journal,* vol. 32, no. 1, 2011. www.family.org.au.

20. Quoted in Monya Baker, "James Thomson: Shifts from Embryonic Stem Cells to Induced Pluripotency," *Nature* Reports: Stem Cells, August 14, 2008. www.nature.com.

21. Quoted in Sally Lehrman, "Dolly's Creator Moves Away from Cloning and Embryonic Stem Cells," *Scientific American,* July 22, 2008. www.scientificamerican.com.

22. Monya Baker, "Court Lifts Cloud over Embryonic Stem Cells," *Nature*, January 2013. www.nature.com.

23. Bradley J. Fikes, "UCSD Team Invents Brain Cell Breakthrough," *San Diego Union-Tribune,* January 10, 2013. www.utsandiego.com.

24. Matt Bowman, "Embryonic Stem Cells: Outmoded Science," CNN.com, September 16, 2010. www.cnn.com.

25. Quoted in Sarah Boseley, "Stem Cell Scientists Take Hope from First Human Trials," *Guardian* (London), June 4, 2012. www.guardian.co.uk.

26. Ed Fallone, "A Status Report on Stem Cell Research," Wisconsin Stem Cell Now, October 3, 2012. www.wistemcellnow.org.

27. International Society for Stem Cell Research, "Stem Cell Science Leaders Congratulate Shinya Yamanaka and John Gurdon for the 2012 Nobel Prize and Reaffirm Their Support for All Forms of Stem

Cell Research Including Human Embryonic Stem Cells," October 11, 2012. www.isscr.org.

28. Goldstein and Schneider, *Stem Cells for Dummies*, p. 293.

29. Quoted in Sharon Begley, "Still No Truce in the Stem Cell Wars," *Newsweek*, February 10, 2010. www.dailybeast.com.

30. Michael D. West, "ES and iPS Cells: Which Holds the Future of Biotechnology?," Biotime, July 26, 2010. www.biotimeinc.com.

31. Baker, "Court Lifts Cloud over Embryonic Stem Cells."

32. Quoted in Baker, "Court Lifts Cloud over Embryonic Stem Cells."

33. Francis Collins, testimony before the U.S. Senate, Subcommittee on Labor, Health and Human Service, and Education, and Related Agencies, Committee on Appropriations, hearing on "The Promise of Human Embryonic Stem Cell Research," US Government Printing Office Federal Digital System, September 16, 2010, p. 8.

34. George Q. Daley, testimony before the U.S. Senate, Subcommittee on Labor, Health and Human Service, and Education, and Related Agencies, Committee on Appropriations, hearing on "The Promise of Human Embryonic Stem Cell Research," US Government Printing Office Federal Digital System, September 16, 2010, p. 39.

35. Daley, testimony before the U.S. Senate, p. 38.

Chapter Three: Should the Federal Government Fund Embryonic Stem Cell Research?

36. Daley, testimony before the U.S. Senate, p. 39.

37. Quoted in Meredith Wadman, "Court Quashes Stem Cell Lawsuit," *Nature*, August 2, 2011. www.nature.com.

38. Stem Cell Action Coalition, "Talking Points for Stem Cell Research," 2010. http://stemcellaction.org.

39. Quoted in Claudia Kalb, "A New Stem Cell Era," Daily Beast, March 8, 2009. www.thedailybeast.com.

40. Goldstein and Schneider, *Stem Cells for Dummies*, p. 276.

41. Robert Streiffer, "Obama's Guidelines on Human Stem Cell Research: Expanding Funding, Improving Oversight," *Bioethics Forum* (blog), the Hasting Center, July 16, 2009. www.thehastingscenter.org.

42. *USA Today*, "Bush Remarks on Stem Cell Research," June 20, 2007. www.usatoday.com.

43. Quoted in Goldstein and Schneider, *Stem Cells for Dummies,* p. 55.

44. Roger Wicker, testimony before the U.S. Senate, Subcommittee on Labor, Health and Human Service, and Education, and Related Agencies, Committee on Appropriations, hearing on "The Promise of Human Embryonic Stem Cell Research," US Government Printing Office Federal Digital System, September 16, 2010, p. 8.

45. James Sherley, "NIH, Do the Right Thing," *Daily Caller*, October 7, 2010. http://dailycaller.com.

46. Michael Fumento, "The Great Stem Cell Research Scam," *New York Post*, July 15, 2009, http://fumento.com.

47. Sigrid Fry-Revere and Molly Elgin, "Public Stem Cell Research Funding: Boon or Boondoggle?," Competitive Enterprise Institute, September 3, 2008. http://cei.org.

48. Fry-Revere and Elgin, "Public Stem Cell Research Funding."

49. Quoted in Gene Tarnes, "The Ethical Stems of Good Science," Charlotte Lozier Institute, July 12, 2012. www.lozierinstitute.org.

Chapter Four: Are More Government Regulations Needed for Stem Cell Research?

50. Ferris Jabr, "Stem Cell Therapy Wasn't Unfair Help for Baseball Star," *New Scientist,* June 8, 2011. www.newscientist.com.

51. Quoted in John Farrell, "One Man's Reluctant Tour for Adult Stem Cells," Forbes.com, February 21, 2013. www.forbes.com.

52. Quoted in Keith Lockitch, "Will the FDA Choke Off Promising Adult Stem Cell Research?," *Daily Caller,* August 10, 2012. www .dailycaller.com.

53. Lockitch, "Will the FDA Choke Off Promising Adult Stem Cell Research?"

54. Scott Gottlieb and Coleen Klasmeier, "The FDA Wants to Regulate Your Cells," *Wall Street Journal*, August 8, 2012. www.aei.org.

55. Gottlieb and Klasmeier, "The FDA Wants to Regulate Your Cells."

56. David Cyranoski, "Stem Cells Boom in Vet Clinics," *Nature*, April 11, 2013. www.nature.com.

57. Quoted in Cyranoski, "Stem Cells Boom in Vet Clinics."

58. Quoted in Farrell, "One Man's Reluctant Tour for Adult Stem Cells."

59. Marcia Heroux Pounds, "Patients Seek Stem-Cell 'Miracle,' But Scientists Warn of Dangers," Fort Lauderdale (FL) *Sun-Sentinel*, January 3, 2013. www.sun-sentinel.com.

60. CBS News, "Stem Cell Fraud: A *60 Minutes* Investigation," January 8, 2012. www.cbsnews.com.

61. Gergana Koleva, "Stem Cells, FDA, and the Edge of Science: Three Expert Viewpoints," Forbes.com, February 19, 2012. www.forbes.com.

62. Quoted in David Cyranoski, "FDA's Claims over Stem Cells Upheld," *Nature*, July 27, 2012. www.nature.com.

63. Quoted in Cyranoski, "FDA's Claims over Stem Cells Upheld."

64. Robin L. Smith, "Understanding FDA Oversight of Cell Therapies," *Genetic Engineering & Biotechnology News,* vol. 32, no. 20, November 12, 2012. www.genengnews.com.

Stem Cell Research Facts

Stem Cell Characteristics

- Stem cells are totipotent, pluripotent, or multipotent.
- When a sperm cell and an egg cell unite, they form a one-celled fertilized egg. This cell is totipotent, meaning it can form all the cell types in a body. During cell division, totipotent cells begin to specialize into pluripotent and multipotent stem cells.
- Pluripotent stem cells can develop into any type of cell in the body (except those needed to support a fetus in the womb).
- Pluripotent stem cells are derived from a five-day-old embryo (embryonic stem cells) or from a single cell that has been modified to revert back to embryonic-like status (iPS cells).
- Multipotent stem cells can develop into one of a limited number of specialized types of cells. Adult stem cells are multipotent.
- A stem cell line is a group of identical stem cells grown and multiplied in a lab dish; stem cell lines can be frozen in liquid nitrogen for future use.

Types of Adult Stem Cells

- Hematopoietic stem cells are found in bone marrow and give rise to white and red blood cells. They can also be harvested and stored from umbilical cord blood after childbirth.
- Mesenchymal stem cells, also found in bone marrow, can create cells that make up bone, fat, cartilage, and connective tissues.
- Neural stem cells, found in the brain, give rise to neurons and two other specialized cells of the brain and nervous system.
- At least 60 percent of all differentiated cells in the body are epithelial cells; epithelial tissues, such as skin, contain stem cells that are capable of self-renewal and differentiation.

Public Funding of Stem Cell Research

- As of January 2013 the NIH had 198 ESC lines on its registry, up from 21 in 2009.

- According to the Stem Cell Action Coalition, more than two hundred human ESC research projects, supporting thirteen hundred jobs, receive NIH funding.

- States that have funded stem cell research, including ESC research, include California, Connecticut, Maryland, New Jersey, and New York.

- States that have banned or restricted funding of ESC research include Arizona, Virginia, South Dakota, and Louisiana.

- In 2013 Kansas established an adult stem cell research center; the new facility would be forbidden to use ESCs.

- About 70 percent of the $1 billion in annual NIH funding for stem cells goes to adult stem cell research.

Stem Cells in Medical Treatments

- As of 2013 there were no FDA-licensed stem cell treatments apart from bone marrow transplants and a similar treatment derived from umbilical cord blood.

- A 2012 clinical trial by the University of Miami Miller School of Medicine found that treating heart attack victims with mesenchymal stem cells reduced heart scar tissue by 33 percent.

- There are more than seven hundred clinics worldwide that offer some sort of stem cell treatments, according to an April 2012 article in *Developing World Bioethics.*

- According to journalist Eliza Barclay of *National Geographic News*, the average cost for stem cell therapy/treatment is around $21,000, with some clinics charging as much as $70,000.

- A recent popular trend in plastic surgery is the "stem cell facelift," in which fatty tissue (which includes stem cells) is taken from the patient's stomach and injected into the patient's face.

The Possible Effects on Health Care Costs

- According to the FDA, using cultured tissues derived from stem cells could save $100 million annually by increasing the efficiency and accuracy of drug testing.
- According to the Stem Cell Action Coalition, research on human ESCs could save $250 billion in annual US health care costs if its potential to treat heart failure, diabetes, and other diseases is realized.

Related Organizations and Websites

California Institute for Regenerative Medicine (CIRM)
210 King St.
San Francisco, CA 94107
phone: (415) 396-9100 • fax: (415) 396-9141
e-mail: info@cirm.ca.gov • website: www.cirm.ca.gov

CIRM is a state-funded organization that seeks to further all types of human stem cell research through grants and public education programs. Its website includes articles and videos providing information on stem cells and research projects in California.

Coalition for the Advancement of Medical Research (CAMR)
750 Seventeenth St. NW, Suite 1100
Washington, DC 20006
phone: (202) 725-0339
e-mail: CAMResearch@yahoo.com • website: www.camradvocacy.org

The CAMR comprises more than one hundred patient organizations, universities, and foundations and engages in advocacy and education outreach focusing on biomedical research. It supports the funding of human ESC research.

Do No Harm: The Coalition of Americans for Research Ethics
1100 H St. NW, Suite 700
Washington, DC 20005
phone: (202) 347-6840 • fax: (202) 347-6849
e-mail: media@stemcellresearch.org • websites: www.stemcellresearch.org and www.stemcellresearchfacts.org

Do No Harm is an organization composed of scientists, researchers, and concerned individuals who oppose human ESC research for ethical reasons and promote the use of adult stem cells and iPS cells. Its websites contain articles on stem cell research issues and personal testimonials of patients helped by adult stem cell treatments.

Harvard Stem Cell Institute (HSCI)

Holyoke Center, Suite 727W
1350 Massachusetts Ave.
Cambridge, MA 02138
phone: (617) 496-4050
e-mail: hsci@harvard.edu • website: www.hsci.harvard.edu

The HSCI, founded in 2004, is a collaborative network of stem cell scientists connected with Harvard University, its affiliated hospitals, and other institutions. It seeks to support and accelerate embryonic and adult stem cell research and regenerative medicine. Its website includes a glossary and other materials and links regarding stem cell research and public policy.

International Society for Stem Cell Research (ISSCR)

5215 Old Orchard Rd., Suite 270
Skokie, IL 60077
phone: (224) 592-5700 • fax: (224) 365-0004
e-mail: isscr@isscr.org • website: www.isscr.org

The ISSCR is a private, nonprofit organization established to foster the exchange and dissemination of information on stem cell research and promote education in all areas of stem cell research and its application. Its website includes the online newsletter the *Pulse* and the downloadable ISSCR Patient Handbook on Stem Cell Therapies.

National Institutes of Health (NIH) Resource for Stem Cell Research

9000 Rockville Pike
Bethesda, MD 20892
phone: (301) 496-4000
e-mail: stemcell@mail.nih.gov • website: http://stemcells.nih.gov

The NIH is the primary federal agency responsible for conducting and funding medical research in the United States. It maintains the NIH

Human Embryonic Stem Cell Registry, listing stem cell lines eligible for use in federally-funded research projects. Its Stem Cell Information Home Page is a portal for research reports, ethical issues, and policy statements.

Right to Life of Michigan (RTL)
2340 Porter St. SW
PO Box 901
Grand Rapids, MI 49509-0901
phone: (616) 532-2300 • fax: (616) 532-3461
e-mail: info@rtl.org • website: www.rtl.org and
www.stemcellresearchcures.com

The RTL is a pro-life organization that opposes human ESC research. Its websites provide numerous articles and information sheets on stem cell research issues.

Stem Cell Health Alliance (SCHA)
1104 Camino Del Mar, Suite 14
Del Mar, CA 92014
phone: (858) 875-6568 • fax: (858) 658-0986
e-mail: info@StemCellHealthAlliance.org • website: www.stemcellhealth alliance.org

Founded in 2008 and initially called the World Stem Cell Foundation, the SCHA seeks to provide patients and consumers with accurate and reliable information on stem cells, specifically the use of donated adult stem cells in clinical treatments. Its website features videos and other information on ongoing stem cell research.

For Further Research

Books

Leo Furcht and William Hoffman, *The Stem Cell Dilemma: The Scientific Breakthroughs, Ethical Concerns, Political Tensions, and Hope Surrounding Stem Cell Research*, 2nd ed. New York: Arcade, 2011.

Paul Knoepfler, *Stem Cells: An Insider's Guide*. Hackensack, NJ: World Scientific, 2013.

Alice Park, *The Stem Cell Hope: How Stem Cell Medicine Can Change Our Lives*. New York: Hudson Street, 2011.

Ted Peters et al. *Sacred Cells?: Why Christians Should Support Stem Cell Research*. Lanham, MD: Rowman & Littlefield, 2010.

Bonnie Szumski and Jill Karson, *Is Human Embryo Experimentation Ethical?* San Diego: ReferencePoint, 2012.

Periodicals

Susan Berfield, "Stem Cell Showdown: Celltex vs. the FDA," *Business Week,* January 3, 2013.

Eryn Brown, "Reverting Cells to Their Embryonic State, Without the Embryos," *Los Angeles Times,* November 27, 2010.

Sally Lehrman, "Undifferentiated Ethics: Why Stem Cells from Adult Skin Are as Morally Fraught as Embryonic Stem Cells," *Scientific American,* September 13, 2010.

Nature, "Smoke and Mirrors," April 18, 2013.

Jeffrey M. O'Brien, "The Great Stem Cell Dilemma," *Fortune,* October 8, 2012.

Minjae Park, "Texas Board Approves Rules on Use of Stem Cells," *New York Times,* April 13, 2012.

Valerie Ross, "Stem Cell Research Hits More Painful Setbacks," *Discover,* January/February 2012.

Wesley J. Smith, "All the News That's Fit to Forget: Why You're Not Hearing Much About Embryonic Stem Cells These Days," *Weekly Standard,* November 28, 2011.

Nicholas Wade, "Cloning and Stem Cell Work Earns Nobel," *New York Times,* October 8, 2012.

Internet Sources

Lindsay Abrams, "2013: Year of the Stem Cell," *Atlantic,* December 28, 2012. www.theatlantic.com/health/archive/2012/12/2013-year-of-the-stem-cell/266574.

Neal Goldfarb, "Sherley v. Sebelius: A Win but the Fight Continues," January 2013, Stem Cell Action Coalition. www.stemcellaction.org/content/sherley-v-sebelius-win-fight-continues.

Paul Knoepfler, *Knoepfler Lab Stem Cell Blog.* www.ipscell.com.

Patients for Stem Cells, "How Safe Are Stem Cells?," February 28, 2013. www.patientsforstemcells.org/education/how-safe-are-stem-cells.

Index

Note: Boldface page numbers indicate illustrations.

Aden, Steven H., 45
adult stem cells, 8
　government should fund
　　research using, 48–49
　types of, 53–54, 69

Baker, Monya, 35–36
Barclay, Eliza, 70
Barnard, Justin D., 17
Belmont Report (US Department
　of Health, Education, and
　Welfare), 14–15, 16, 18
blastocysts, 7–8, 19
　numbers of, stored in fertility
　　clinics, 23
Bowman, Matt, 32
Bush, George W., 39, 40–41, 43
　on adoption of frozen embryos,
　　16
　on destruction of human
　　embryos to save lives, 17
　limits placed on ESC research
　　by, 9–10, 42

California Institute for
　Regenerative Medicine, 72
Centeno, Christopher J., 52, 54

Clinton, Bill, 50
cloning
　reproductive versus therapeutic,
　　17
　See also somatic cell nuclear
　　transfer
Coalition for the Advancement of
　Medical Research (CAMR), 72
Collins, Francis S., 36
Colón, Bartolo, 52–53
Cyranoski, David, 56

Daley, George Q., 36, 37, 41
Decision Points (Bush), 17
Department of Health, Education,
　and Welfare, US, 14–15, 16, 18
Developing World Bioethics
　(journal), 70
Dickey, Jay, 46
Dickey, Roger, 46
Dickey-Wicker Amendment
　(1995), 8, 42–43, 46, 48
Do No Harm: The Coalition of
　Americans for Research Ethics,
　72

Eckland, Dan, 60
Elgin, Molly, 49–50
embryonic stem cell research
　ethics of, debate over, 12

government funding of, debate
   over, 38
government should fund, 39–44
government should not fund,
   45–46, 49–50
guidelines for, 20–22
is ethical, 19–20
is necessary, 32–37
is no longer necessary, 26–31
is unethical, 13–17
necessity of, debate over, 25
reasons for disapproval of, **15**
restrictions on, 8–10
support for government funding
   of, 46, **47**
embryonic stem cells (ESCs), 7,
   19–20
   advantages of, **35**
   versus induced pluripotent stem
      cells, **28,** 29
embryos, human
   adoption of, 16–17
   religious differences on moral
      standing of, 22
epithelial cells, 69
ESCs. *See* embryonic stem cells

Fallone, Ed, 33
Faulkner, Stephen, 52
Fikes, Bradley J., 30
Finger, Reginald, 16
Food and Drug Administration
   (FDA), 54–55, 59, 71
   importance of regulation by, 51,
      61–63

Fry-Revere, Sigrid, 49–50
Fumento, Michael, 49, 50

Grekos, Zannos, 60
Goldstein, Lawrence S.B., 23,
   33–34, 42
Gottlieb, Scott, 55

Harvard Stem Cell Institute, 73
Hemacord, 59
hematopoietic stem cells, 53, 69
Hilton, Marcus, 33
Hyan, Insoo, 22

induced pluripotent stem (iPS)
   cells, 11, 18
   advantages of, versus embryonic
      stem cells, **28,** 29
   need for benchmarks on,
      35–36
   potential problems with,
      34–35
International Society for Stem
   Cell Research, 20, 32, 33
in vitro fertilization (IVF), 16

Jabr, Ferris, 53

Kerr, Candace, 41
Klasmeier, Coleen, 55
Koleva, Gergana, 60–61
Kurtzburg, Joanne, 60

Lanza, Robert, 33, 34
Layton, John R., 39

Lockitch, Keith, 54–55

mesenchymal stem cells, 53, 69
multipotent stem cells, 69

National Academy of Sciences, 20
National Bioethics Advisory Commission, 50
National Institutes of Health (NIH), 10, 44
    guidelines for research funded by, 20–22
    number of ESC lines on registry of, 70
    on plasticity of stem cells, 7
    role of, in medical research, 40
neural stem cells, 53, 69
NIH. *See* National Institutes of Health
Nordone, Shila, 57

Obama, Barack, 10, 39–40, 43–44, 46
opinion polls. *See* surveys
Oregon Science and Health University, 29

Panno, Joseph, 14
Pederson, Roger, 41
Pelley, Scott, 59–60
Pence, Mike, 26
Phelan, Michael, 53, 57
pluripotent stem cells, 18, 69
    definition of, 11, 20

See also induced pluripotent stem cells
polls. *See* surveys
Pounds, Marcia Heroux, 59

Rao, Mehendra, 30
Regenerative Science, 54
Rick, Amy Comstock, 42
Right to Life of Michigan, 13

Savulescu, Julian, 6, 7
Schneider, Meg, 23
Sherley, James, 49
Sherley v. Sebelius (2013), 48, 49
Sipp, Douglas, 58
60 Minutes (TV program), 59–60
Smith, Robin L., 63
somatic cell nuclear transfer (SCNT), 17
Stem Cell Action Coalition, 19, 41, 70, 71
stem cell facelift, 70
Stem Cell Health Alliance, 74
stem cell lines, 69
stem cell research
    ethical forms of, 18
    government regulations are hampering, 52–57
    government should regulate, 58–63
    need for more government regulation of, debate over, 51
    number of clinical trials registered with NIH database, **62**

states funding/banning, 70
stem cells
  characteristics of, 6–7, 69
  types of, 7–8
  See also specific types
stem cell therapy, 70
  for animals, 55–57
  government should carefully
    regulate, 58–63
  health care costs and, 71
  human trials of, 33
  online scams for, 59–60
  risks of, 60–61
    by type of stem cell, **56**
Stem Tech Labs, 60
Streiffer, Robert, 44
surveys
  on ethics of stem cell research,
    21
  on federal funding of ESC
    research, **43**, 46, **47**
  on reasons for opposing ESC
    research, **15**
Susser, Adam, 58–59
Susser, Gary, 58, 60

Susser, Judy, 58, 60

Thomson, James A., 23, 26, 27,
  45
Trevino, Andres, 23, 24
Trevino, Andy, 23–24
Trevino, Paulina, 23, 24
trophoblasts, 19–20
Turner, Leigh, 63

umbilical cord blood, 18, 59
United States Conference of
  Catholic Bishops (USCCB), 47
University of Miami Miller School
  of Medicine, 70

van Gend, David, 29
Vet-Stem, 56

West, Michael D., 34–35
Wicker, Roger, 48
Wilmut, Ian, 30

Yamanaka, Shinya, 6, 7, **9,** 27
Yockey, John, 16